SHAKESPEARE AND SIR PHILIP SIDNEY

THE INFLUENCE OF

The Defense of Poesy

SHAKESPEARE
AND
SIR PHILIP SIDNEY

THE INFLUENCE OF
The Defense of Poesy

BY
ALWIN THALER

NEW YORK / RUSSELL & RUSSELL

TO

Richard Winston Thaler

PREFACE

In the quick forge and working house of thought which was the mind of Shakespeare, many diverse elements were strangely and wonderfully fused. This essay calls attention to one of these elements which has not previously been recognized, though it is clearly important — if true. The possibility that it might be true — that Shakespeare's plays and poems demonstrably reflect the influence of Sidney's *Defense of Poesy* — first occurred to me almost ten years ago, when I was studying Shakespeare's utterances on style, imagination, and poetry. Then and later one question troubled me. If the work of the greatest of the Elizabethans was indeed indebted to the most eloquent and influential piece of literary criticism produced in his time, why has this fact — or even this possibility — virtually escaped notice for over three hundred years? I have attempted to answer this question in the first section of my essay. But the nub of the matter, the proof of the pudding, is the evidence. However this may be interpreted, it can hardly be ignored. I have tried to present it fairly and comprehensively, in the belief that the question here raised demands careful consideration of all pertinent data. The method of this presentation is set forth on pages 3–15. The major implications of the evidence, and some of its bearings upon Shakespearean criticism in general, are summarized in the Concluding Note.

Meanwhile a preliminary note may be in order with regard to one of the basic principles illustrated by this evidence. It is the principle — the bald fact — that some poets, like some elephants, have long memories. Shakespearean illustrations are supplied below. But, in order to point the way if not the moral, I will not resist the temptation to cite, here and now, two or three modern instances.

Shelley, who knew that poets remember, began his sonnet on "England in 1819" with an excoriation of George the Third: "An *old, mad, blind,* despised, and dying king." Two years later, when King George had gone to his reward, Shelley's friend Byron took up the cudgels, literally — for *The Vision of Judgment* (stanza 42) echoes Shelley's sentiment in no uncertain terms. "Look to the earth," says Byron's Satan,

> When this *old, blind, mad,* helpless, weak, poor worm
> Began in youth's first bloom and flush to reign. . . .

If Byron was the borrower in this case, Shelley, for his part, also had a poet's memory. Long ago, Dr. Johnson, in the tenth chapter of *Rasselas,* had written eloquently of the high service poets render to mankind. "To a poet nothing can be useless. Whatever is beautiful and whatever is dreadful must be familiar to his imagination. . . . He must write as the interpreter of nature, and the *legislator of mankind.*" Shelley, it is clear, remembered this injunction in fact and in phrase, for his *Defense of Poetry* ends with the ringing pronouncement that "Poets are . . . the trumpets which sing to battle. . . . Poets are the *unacknowledged legislators of the world.*" Shelley, finally, was probably not the only poet of his time who read Dr. Johnson and perhaps remembered him. Witness the memorable passage in *Tintern Abbey* concerning

> *that best* portion of *a good man*'s life,
> His *little,* nameless, unremembered *acts*
> *Of kindness* and of love.

I, for one, cannot read this passage without recalling Dr. Johnson's dictum to Mrs. Thrale: "Life is made up of little things; and *that character* is *best* which does *little* but repeated *acts of beneficence*" (Hester Lynch Piozzi, *Anecdotes of Samuel Johnson*, ed. S. C. Roberts, 1932, p. 60).

I am grateful to the Syndics and the editorial staff of the Harvard University Press, to Professor James B. Munn, Dean Edwin R. Hunter, and especially to Professor Hyder E. Rollins for sundry acts of kindness; and to my colleagues and other friends — not to mention certain persons still nearer home — for good counsel and suggestions embodied in this study.

CONTENTS

I

WHYS AND WHEREFORES   3

I I

DEFENSE: PART THREE   14

I I I

DEFENSE: PART ONE   34

I V

DEFENSE: PART TWO   66

CONCLUDING NOTE   72

NOTES   75

INDEX   94

SHAKESPEARE AND SIR PHILIP SIDNEY

THE INFLUENCE OF
The Defense of Poesy

THERE ARE MANY MYSTERIES CONTAINED IN
POETRY WHICH OF PURPOSE WERE WRITTEN
DARKLY, LEST BY PROFANE WITS IT SHOULD BE
ABUSED.

SIDNEY, *The Defense of Poesy* [1595]

❧{ I }❧

WHYS AND WHEREFORES

"Concerning imitation," Roger Ascham [1] reminds us, "many learned men have written . . . with great contrariety and some stomach amongst themselves." [2] Erasmus, in spite of the contrarieties of Renaissance scholarship, wished that some diligent investigator would "write out and join together where" Cicero "doth imitate" Demosthenes. [3] Ascham himself goes on to say that "there is no precept in Aristotle's *Topics* whereof plenty of examples be not manifest in Plato's works." Then follows a pious wish, which, with a change of principals, I shall humbly seek to fulfill in this study: "Would to God I might once see some worthy student . . . that would join in one book the precepts" of Aristotle "with the examples of" Plato. [4] Fifty-odd years ago Professor A. S. Cook prefaced his excellent edition of Sidney's *Defense of Poesy* [5] — otherwise known as *An Apology for Poetry* — with the remark that "what Sidney outlined, Spenser and Shakespeare executed, though not always in the precise forms which he himself would have approved." So far as I know, however, no one has yet attempted to join in one comprehensive study the precepts of the greatest of the Elizabethan critics with the examples of the mighty poet whose career began soon after Sidney's death in 1586. I make this attempt here. That no one seems to have made it hitherto is understandable, in one sense. In

Sidney's *Arcadia* and in his *Astrophel and Stella* students have long since found materials upon which Shakespeare drew in writing *King Lear,* the sonnets, and perhaps some of his other plays.[6] But what stories or poetic themes could Shakespeare possibly have drawn from a mere critical tractate, *The Defense of Poesy?* I suggest, in reply, that a reading of Sidney's eloquent essay could hardly have failed to delight, or at least to challenge, Shakespeare's own critical sense. If so, however, why has not this answer occurred to others long before now? I venture two explanations. First, Shakespearean criticism has had many other questions to answer. Second, ever since Milton's time, and long after Carlyle's and Emerson's, the majority of readers have accepted too readily the legendary half-truth that Shakespeare, "Fancy's child," was the great exemplar of vitally spontaneous genius, "unconscious" of art and unconcerned with criticism. Whatever the explanation, the main question so far proposed here — whether or not Sidney's essay specifically influenced Shakespeare's work — will require closer attention shortly. For the moment I suggest merely that the failure to put together Sidney's precepts and Shakespeare's practice has kept critics, commentators, and editors — Sidney's as well as Shakespeare's [7] — from recognizing many significant points of contact between the two poets; at the very least, many useful illustrations of Elizabethan idiom in thought and word. In analyzing, later, the chief elements of Sidney's treatise, I shall cite chapter and verse systematically to substantiate the view that almost every major idea or principle in the *Defense* can be illustrated in some measure by Shakespeare's practice. Meanwhile, a few preliminary illustrations of four different kinds will indicate the desirability of a comprehensive study of Shakespeare's utterances in the light of Sidney's prophetic [8] doctrine.

First: Several of Sidney's editors [9] have noted that one of his most eloquent passages won the immediate admiration of his contemporaries — so much so that Harington quoted it in his *Brief Apology* (1591) four years before Sidney's work was printed.[10] It is the passage in which Sidney holds that the poet's teaching excels the philosopher's, because it substitutes for abstract "particularities . . . . words . . . in delightful proportion . . . the well enchanting skill of music," and a story: "With a tale forsooth he cometh unto you, with a tale which holdeth children from play, and old men from the chimney corner." [11] Sidney's editors underscore Harington's use of this passage, but hardly any of the editors, Sidney's or Shakespeare's,[12] mention the strikingly similar passage in *Love's Labour's Lost* (II, i, 72–76). Rosaline is the speaker, and her subject is the mirthful Berowne's "sweet" and "voluble" poetic discourse. His "fair tongue (conceit's expositor)" utters

> such apt and gracious words
> That *aged ears play truant at his tales*
> And *younger hearings are quite ravished*.

Another: For preliminary notice also, I submit another instance — emphatically marked by both our poets — of their oft-repeated insistence upon the fact that one of the most important gifts of the true poet is the art of telling a good story. "The austere admonitions of the philosopher," to quote Sidney again, are humanized by the delightful tales of "the good fellow, poet." Instance: "The one of Menenius Agrippa," who, when the Roman plebs were rebellious, "behave[d] himself like a homely and familiar poet." Let us

6

set side by side Sidney's account [13] of Menenius's behavior, and Shakespeare's version as recorded in *Coriolanus*.

According to Sir Philip, Menenius met the emergency with the quick instinct of a true poet. *"He telleth them a tale,"* one of these unforgettably *"pretty* tales" [14] of the poets, as Sidney describes them a moment later. The tale of Menenius, in sum, comes to this: *"There was a time when all the parts of the body made a mutinous* conspiracy against the belly . . . they concluded they would let so unprofitable a spender starve. . . ."*

Coriolanus, I, i, 92–153 (Menenius speaking to the plebeians):

I shall tell you
A *pretty tale.*

There was a time when all the body's members
Rebell'd against the belly; thus accus'd it:
That only like a gulf it did remain
I' th' midst o' th' body, idle and unactive . . .

The senators of Rome are this good belly,
And you the *mutinous* members.

. . . th' discontented members, the *mutinous* parts. [15]

In discussing Shakespeare's sources and analogues for this ancient and wide-spread fable, [16] Chambers and Furness [17] do not mention Sidney's version at all. Sidney's editors do somewhat better — that is to say, several of them annotate the passage in the *Defense* with the suggestion "Cf. Shakespeare, *Coriolanus*." [18] But none of them, to my knowledge, has observed that this is still another "pretty tale" told by a poet to keep children from play, or mischief, and that Shakespeare's lines are, on the whole, closer to Sidney's than to any one of the other sources hitherto suggested: [19] in the identical phrasing of the opening clause (*"There was a time when all the . . ."*) and in the twice repeated adjective "mutinous."

A third example: "Good phrases," says Shallow,[20] "are surely, and ever were, very commendable." All good Elizabethans loved good phrases, Sidney and Shakespeare not least of all. Of course Sir Philip protested that he was no pickpurse of another's wit, but a good phrase was another matter: witness *Astrophel and Stella* and the *Defense* itself.[21] As for Shakespeare: "The way in which Shakespeare picked up phrases" [22] is as baffling — and as clear and open — as the way of a maid with a man. To illustrate, I submit another group of Shakespearean phrases which seem not far removed from Sidney's in the *Defense*.

(a) *Defense* (Smith, I, 199): The ancients . . . . never, or very daintily, match *hornpipes and funerals*. . . . Comedy should be full of *delight* . . . tragedy . . . still maintained in a well raised *admiration*.

Hamlet, I, ii, 12–13: With *mirth* in *funeral*, and with *dirge* in *marriage*, In equal scale weighing *delight* and *dole*.
[Cf. Cook, p. 123.]

(b) *Defense* (Smith, I, 177): High and excellent tragedy . . . openeth the greatest wounds and showeth forth the *ulcers* that are *covered with tissue*.
[Cf. below, p. 15.]

Hamlet, III, iv, 145–150: Lay not that flattering unction to your soul. . . . It will but *skin and film* the *ulcerous place*, Whiles rank corruption, mining all within, Infects unseen.
[Cf. Cook, p. 96.]

(c) *Defense* (Smith, I, 187): I yield that poesie . . . being abused, by the reason of his sweet charming force . . . can

Merchant of Venice, III, v, 48, 71–72: How every fool can play upon the word!

do more hurt than any other
army of words.[23]

The fool hath planted in his
memory
An *army of good words.*

But good phrases, however commendable, are not the whole
story.

My fourth illustration will serve to test the hypothesis that
Shakespeare may have remembered more than an occasional
phrase of Sidney's. In an earlier study [24] I pointed out that
Shakespeare, like Sidney, frequently emphasizes the importance of the creative imagination. At that writing, however,
I had not studied Sidney with close reference to Shakespeare.
At any rate, I then missed (like everyone else, so far as I
have been able to discover) what now seems to me a striking
series of likenesses between two of the most familiar passages
in Shakespeare — the lines on the poetic imagination in *A
Midsummer Night's Dream* — and Sidney's eloquent dis-
quisition on the same general subject in the *Defense.* Within
their limits, these passages (with others in kind, to be mentioned later) [25] mark Sidney's and Shakespeare's claims for
a place in the ranks of England's poet-critics, as predecessors
of Wordsworth, Coleridge, Shelley, and Matthew Arnold.

(a) 1. *Defense* (Smith, I,
169):

Whatsoever action . . . the historian . . . recite[s], that may
the poet . . . make his own . . .
having all, *from* Dante his
heaven to his *hell,* under . . .
his *pen.*

2. (Smith, I, 165):
[Philosophical definitions] lie
dark before the *imaginative*

A Midsummer Night's Dream,
V, i, 7–18:

The lunatic, the lover, and
the poet
Are of *imagination all compact*
. . . .
The poet's eye, in a fine frenzy
rolling,
Doth glance from *heaven to
earth, from earth to heaven;*
And as imagination *bodies
forth*

and judging power, if they be not . . . *figured forth* by the speaking picture of *poesy.*

    3. (Smith, I, 156):
Only the poet, disdaining to be tied to any . . . subjection, *lifted up* with the vigor of his own invention, doth [make] . . . *forms such as never were* in nature.

    4. (Smith, I, 185):
The poets *give names* . . . to make their picture the more lively.

(b) (Smith, I, 185):
The poet never maketh any circles about your *imagination,* to conjure you *to believe for true* what he writes . . . . the poet's persons and doings *are but pictures* . . . allegorically and *figuratively* written.[26]

The *forms of things unknown,* the poet's *pen* Turns them to shapes, and *gives* to *airy nothing* A local habitation and *a name.* Such tricks hath strong imagination.

A Midsummer Night's Dream, V, i, 214–217:
The best in this kind *are but shadows,* and the worst are no worse, if *imagination* amend them.

Macbeth, II, ii, 53–54:
The sleeping and the dead *are but as pictures.*

    "Among moderns," writes Professor Cook,[27] "it is difficult to believe that Shelley was ignorant of Sidney's tractate, though the similarities of opinion may be due to familiarity with common sources . . . or to the deeper insight of which genius alone is capable." This caveat must not be forgotten. (It might be argued, for example, that "familiarity with common sources" — such as Horace's *Ars Poetica* [28] — may account for some likenesses between Sidney and Shakespeare.) Professor N. I. White's recent research,[29] however, has definitely substantiated Cook's belief that Shelley knew

the *Defense*. By the same token, it is difficult to believe, even
in the face of the fragmentary evidence thus far presented,
that Shakespeare was ignorant of Sidney's work. "Poets,"
said Shelley, "the best of them, are a very camœleonic race;
they take the colour not only of what they feed on, but of the
very leaves under which they pass." [30] As for the Elizabethans, everyone who knows anything about them knows that
they — critics and poets — were inveterate borrowers from
one another. If Shakespeare had written a systematic treatise
on poetics he could not possibly have escaped the influence of
the *Defense*. "Each critic, like each poet," says Gregory
Smith,[31] "might well suspect his neighbor"; and he proves
that Sidney's work was "known to everybody and cited by
nearly all" the Elizabethan critics. Though Shakespeare certainly did not write a systematic critique of poetry, it would
have been almost impossible for him to be ignorant of the
Defense, if only because he was a player, a poet, and a playwright. As already indicated, he certainly knew the *Arcadia*
and *Astrophel and Stella*. Knowing these works, how could
the young poet-dramatist, who apparently read everything
in sight, have failed to read the most trenchant and univer-
sally quoted dramatic criticism written in his time —that of
the *Defense?* Particularly so in view of the fact that Sidney
was well known to the players, specifically to Leicester's men,
with whom Shakespeare may have begun his career? Witness Sidney's letter to Walsingham written on March 24,
1586, not long before his death, which has been thought to
allude to Shakespeare's fellow, Will Kemp: "I wrote to you
a letter by Will, my Lord of Leicester's jesting player." [32]
Nor are Shakespeare's contacts with the *Defense* limited to
these general probabilities. Not only the critics knew it; but

also the poets. Among the former, Puttenham and Florio —
like Harington — alluded to it even before, and Francis
Meres soon after, its publication.[33] As for the poets,[34] men
of such varied calibre as Thomas Churchyard and Michael
Drayton, Spenser and Vaughan and Wither, Thomas Nashe
and Ben Jonson, praised or imitated Sidney's essay. For our
purposes, Ben Jonson's repeated and unequivocal allusions to
the *Defense of Poesy* deserve special notice.

The point is, of course, that the author of *Every Man in
His Humour*, in which Shakespeare acted, was not only
Shakespeare's friend and fellow playwright but also his cope-
mate in the famous wit-combats at the Mermaid [35] which, in
the nature of things, could not have failed to touch upon
"divine Sir Philip's" strictures against the irregularities of
early Elizabethan drama.[36] As regards Jonson and the
Defense, scholars have indicated at least four sets of contacts.
Spingarn,[37] for example, observes that Jonson's definition of
poetry in *Timber* is substantially in keeping with Sidney's,
and another investigator [38] has suggested that Jonson's attack
upon "Poet-Apes" in *The Poetaster* repeats Sidney's: "the
cause why [poesy] is not esteemed in England is the fault of
poet-apes, not poets." More definitely conclusive are Jonson's allusions to Sidney's treatise in the Prologue to *Every
Man in His Humour* and in the second act of *The Silent
Woman*. The Prologue unmistakably harks back to Sidney's
attack upon the early dramatists' "faulty" disregard of the
unities of "place and time," their stage children whose children and grandchildren are begotten "in two hours' space,"
their "hideous monster[s]," and their crude stage "armies
. . . represented with four swords and bucklers." These

"gross absurdities" of Sidney's stage [39] Jonson matches in his excoriation of the "ill customs" of his "age":

> To make a child, now swaddled, to . . . shoot up . . .
> Past three score years; or, with three rusty swords . . .
> Fight over York and Lancaster's long jars.

He will have no truck with stage "monsters":

> But deeds, and language, such as men do use,
> And persons, such as Comedy would choose,
> When she would show an image of the times,
> And sport with human follies, not with crimes. [40]

In *The Silent Woman* Dauphine and Clerimont bait Sir John Daw: "Every man that writes in verse is not a poet; you hail of the wits that write verses and yet are not poets." (Sidney had written: "It is not rhyming and versing that maketh poesy. One may be a poet without versing, and a versifier without poetry.") [41] The exchange of views in *The Silent Woman* concludes as follows: "A knight live by his verses? . . . The noble Sidney lives by his." [42]

Our case so far, then, would seem to stand as follows. At first glance, sundry passages in Shakespeare are sufficiently close to Sidney's thought and words to justify a comprehensive review of the main sections and arguments of the *Defense* in terms of possible Shakespearean recollection. The antecedent probabilities strongly support the hypothesis that Shakespeare knew and used Sidney's work: because the Elizabethans were inveterate borrowers from one another, because Sidney was well known to the players, and because this particular work of his won not only immediate fame but also left indelible marks upon the memory of the Elizabethan poets, especially upon that of Shakespeare's friend and fellow,

Ben Jonson. Now Sidney's *Defense*, as Spingarn [43] has shown, "is a veritable epitome of the literary criticism of the Italian Renaissance. . . . So thoroughly is it imbued with this spirit that no other work, Italian, French, or English can be said to give so complete and noble a conception of the temper and the principles of Renaissance criticism." I believe the following analysis will substantiate the view that Shakespeare was influenced by Sidney's work. If so, we shall have another good reason [44] for recognizing in Shakespeare's work the achievement of an artist who was familiar with the best critical thought of his age.

DEFENSE: PART THREE

The *Defense of Poesy* falls into three main parts, roughly marked by Sidney's own summaries.[1] But the three parts are not mutually exclusive; indeed there is much overlapping and repetition. The following preliminary analysis[2] will suffice for our purposes. Part One presents Sidney's definitions of poetry, reviews its imaginative, historic, and philosophic background, enumerates rapidly its "kinds or species,"[3] and asserts its claims as the earliest of teachers, the mirror of nature, and, in various respects, the superior of history and philosophy. Part Two analyzes and refutes the various "objections" made against this art by the "poet-haters" — Stephen Gosson and his tribe. Part Three inquires "why England" has "grown so hard a stepmother to poetry," touches upon earlier and contemporary English poets, and discusses in some detail the defects of the English drama. It then examines current affectations in the lyric, in prose style, and diction, and closes with an excursus upon the English language and English versification.

Concerning this third part — especially with regard to its central subject, "our tragedies and comedies" — Sidney himself writes: "I have lavished out too many words of this play matter. I do it because as they are excelling parts of poesy, so is there none so much used in England, and none can be more pitifully abused."[4] Because this section of the *Defense*, besides having to do with "the excelling parts of poesy," is of most immediate concern to the student of Shakespeare, I shall start [5] with it, reserving Parts One and Two for later consideration. But in discussing the items under all the captions which follow, I shall also draw upon closely related materials from other parts of the *Defense*.

Of Tragedy in Sidney and Shakespeare: function; enumeration and differentiation of "kinds"; "laws" and proprieties.

"High and excellent tragedy" had been the subject of Sidney's praise even in the first part of his treatise. It "openeth," he says, "the greatest wounds, and showeth forth the ulcers that are covered with tissue"; it "maketh kings fear to be tyrants, and tyrants manifest their tyrannical humors," [6] — for example, as Shakespeare's Richard III did, according to Milton's observation in the *Eikonoklastes*.[7] Again, according to the *Defense*, "with stirring the effects of admiration and commiseration, [it] teacheth the uncertainty of this world, and upon how weak foundations guilden roofs are builded" [8] — that is to say, in Shakespeare's words, how "they that stand high have many blasts to shake them," how "princes have but their titles for their glories," and how "uneasy lies the head that wears a crown." [9] Certain it is that both poets make much of that function of tragedy which holds the mirror up to tyranny, to make it shudder at its own ugly image. "Poetry," Sidney wrote, "not content with earthly plagues, deviseth new punishments in hell for tyrants." [10] More specifically, he tells of "certain poets" who "so prevailed with Hiero the First, that of a tyrant they made him a just king," and he remembers another "abominable tyrant" who was so moved by "a tragedy, well made and represented" that "in despite of himself" he "withdrew himself from harkening." [11] One recalls still another guilty creature at a play, a king named Claudius, who did the same thing when the "mousetrap" was sprung in *Hamlet*, though it is true enough that Sidney's tyrant did not supply the one and only Elizabethan precedent for Claudius' action.[12] At all events, it is worth noting that in *Love's Labour's Lost*, a play already mentioned here in connection with Sidney's work, the well-graced Berowne praises a true poet whose

> lines would ravish savage ears
> And *plant in tyrants* mild humility.[13]

Nor does one forget that the tragedy of *Macbeth* is, in a sense, a full length mirror for tyranny, somewhat as *Henry V* is "the mirror of all Christian kings." [14] For example, it was the "tyrant" Macbeth who battered at the peace of Macduff's wife and children until he finally left them "well at peace." Vercors in *The Silence of the Sea* [15] significantly makes the German officer of the story, in spite of himself, allude to his *Führer* by having him quote "a page of *Macbeth* . . . at the end," where one of "the noble lords . . . describes the dramatic portents of . . . the . . . tyrant['s] . . . collapse":

> Now does he feel
> His secret murders sticking on his hands,
> Now minutely revolts upbraid his faith-breach,

and he falls, long before his time, "into the sere, the yellow leaf." [16]

Sidney never tires of stressing the ethical function of poetry in general and of tragedy in particular — the point that "the *ending end* of all earthly learning" is "virtuous action"; that in *Oedipus* we see "all *virtues, vices,* and passions . . . in their own natural seats laid to the view," that *Gorboduc* [17] is praiseworthy for its "notable morality, which it does most delightfully teach, and so obtain *the very end of poesy*." But this moral emphasis must be in accord with, and must set forth the truth of nature. For, according to the pronouncement which Flügel [18] describes as the central thought of the *Defense*, "There is no art delivered to mankind that hath not the works of *nature* for his principal object . . . on which they so depend, as they become *actors and players, as it were,* of what *nature* will have set forth." [19] This basic idea — of drama as a mirror of nature and image of truth — was a commonplace of Renaissance criticism probably derived from Cicero,[20] but it seems altogether probable that Sidney's phrasing of the idea (the "end" of poetry, the mirroring of "nature," of "virtues," "vices," "as it were" by "actors and players") is echoed in Hamlet's remarks on "the purpose of *playing*, whose *end*, both at the first and now . . . is to hold, *as 'twere*, the mirror up to *nature;* to show *virtue* her own feature,[21] scorn her own image, and the very age and body of the time his form and pressure." [22]

Hamlet's remarks suggest a timely glance at other elements of Sidney's analysis of tragedy, also touched upon in the tragedy of the Prince of Denmark: the differentiation of the "kinds and species" of drama, and the discussion of what Sidney, Jonson, and Shakespeare all describe as its "laws." [23]

It seems, for example, not unlikely that Sidney's slightly bookish enumeration of the kinds of poetry: "the heroic, lyric, tragic, comic, satiric, iambic, elegiac, pastoral," [24] and of drama — the "tragical," the "comical," "the tragi-comical," the "mingled . . . heroical and pastoral" [25] — is genially parodied in the portentous list so trippingly pronounced by

that one-time actor of Julius Caesar and later commentator
on the law of writ, the learned Polonius:

> The best actors in the world, either for tragedy, comedy,
> history, pastoral, pastoral-comical, historical-pastoral, tragical-
> historical, tragical-comical-historical-pastoral; scene individ-
> able, or poem unlimited. Seneca cannot be too heavy, nor
> Plautus too light.[26] For the law of writ and the liberty,
> these are the only men.[27]

In connection with Sidney's discussion of tragicomedy [28] we
shall see that Shakespeare shared, in a measure, Sidney's objection to the indiscriminate "mingling" of kinds — of "kings
and clowns" — which had made the early Elizabethan medleys (of the *King Cambyses* school), in Sidney's phrase,
"neither right tragedies nor right comedies." [29] As regards
Elizabethan tragedy, however, I am not sure that Spingarn [30]
is accurate in his flat assertion that whereas "the great Spanish
drama had its critical champions and defenders, the Elizabethan drama had none." The fact is that *Shakespeare's* critical sense finds expression now and then, in defense of his
own work and that of his fellow dramatists, and against certain elements of contemporary critical dogma. Let us con-
sider two or three specific cases.

Polonius's remark concerning "the *law* of writ and the
liberty" clearly indicates, as Professor Kittredge [31] puts it,
that Shakespeare "was well aware of the so-called rules."
Specifically — and significantly, for our purposes — Mr.
Kittredge quotes, in this connection, some of the pertinent
passages from the *Defense*. These are the passages mentioned
above [32] in which Sidney charged the dramatists with being
"faulty" in their disregard of the unities: witness the "liberal"
time allowance for the "two" typical "young princes" of

early Elizabethan drama who, "in two hours' space," meet, beget children, and are ready to greet their grandchildren; and witness also the far-ranging liberty of place which crowded upon one and the same stage "Asia of the one side, and Africa of the other," the while "two armies . . . represented with four swords and bucklers" unconcernedly made "a pitched field" out of these elastic continents. Now Shakespeare, as a rule, does not trouble himself to defend the continental expansiveness of his stage; indeed his practice in so mature a work as *Antony and Cleopatra* shows that, on occasion, he was ready to use this "liberty" for all it was worth.[33] Yet it is all but certain that his practice was neither blindly conceived nor ignorant of sound critical principles. For example (to quote Professor Kittredge once more) the Prologue and Choruses in *King Henry V*

> are interesting documents in the history of dramatic criticism. They express, over and over again, the doctrine of voluntary subjection of our minds to the illusion of the stage . . . a principle which a succession of eminent critics arrived at by a long course of study and debate, and which Schlegel and Coleridge are often thought to have finally worked out.[34]

In the Prologue and in the opening Choruses of Acts II and V, Shakespeare half-apologizes [35] for his temerity in seeking "to cram . . . the vasty fields of France" into the Globe Theatre's small "wooden O." In effect, however, his apology for the obvious crudities of his battle scenes, and for what he calls his "abuse of distance," is less humble than it sounds. Indeed, what he has to say amounts to a confident defense of his practice. "Two Armies [as Sir Philip puts it] . . . represented with four swords and bucklers"? Of course! With-

out the audience's "imaginary puissance" poet and players
would indeed

> Much disgrace
> With four or five most vile and ragged foils,
> Right ill-dispos'd in brawl ridiculous,
> The name of Agincourt.

But the poet counts on the spectators to do their part. "Play
with your fancies!" he says, and in another place: "Piece out
our imperfections with your thoughts." With their imaginative response to aid him, the poet achieves his "great . . .
object": makes good the name of Agincourt and of its royal
captain, Harry, the mirror of all Christian kings. [36]

Shakespeare is even more outspoken in defending his disregard of the unity of time. His reasoning here anticipates
Dr. Johnson,[37] for he urges that the imaginative will to believe sufficiently disposes of all petty objections to the com-
pression of time whereby the dramatist's magic wand turns

> th' accomplishments of many years
> Into an hourglass.[38]

Shakespeare's point is, of course, that stage time — "the two
hours' traffic of our stage" [39] — can move as slowly or as
swiftly as thought and imagination:

> With *imagin'd wing* our swift scene flies,
> In motion of no less celerity
> Than that of thought.

Even more philosophically conclusive in its implied answer to
Sidney's objections, and more immediately pertinent to his
specific complaint of the "two young princes" who grow too
fast, is the speech of Time, the Chorus in the fourth act of
The Winter's Tale:

> I, that please some, try all . . .
> Now take upon me, in the name of Time,
> To use my wings. *Impute it not a crime*
> To me or my swift passage *that I slide*
> *O'er sixteen years* and leave the growth untried
> Of that wide gap, *since it is in my pow'r*
> *To o'erthrow law, and in one self born hour*
> To plant and o'erwhelm custom . . .
>   so shall I do
> To th' freshest things now reigning, and make stale
> The glistering of this present.[40]

In his discussion of the dramatic unities Sidney made another set of observations which Shakespeare, once more,
seems not to have overlooked. The poet's spirit, Sidney had
written, needs "three wings to bear" him up: "art, imitation
and exercise," but the English poets refuse to "cumber"
themselves either with "artificial rules" [41] — i.e., the laws of
poetic art — or with "imitative patterns." [42] Holofernes in
Love's Labour's Lost (IV, ii, 129–131) supports the second
part of this charge, for he says flatly: "Imitari is nothing. So
doth the hound his master, the ape his keeper." "Exercise,"
Sidney continues, the English poets "indeed . . . do, but . . .
very forebackwardly. . . . For, there being two principal
parts, *matter* to be expressed by *words* and *words* to *express
the matter,* in neither we use art or imitation rightly." [43] In
principle, Shakespeare agrees whole-heartedly: that is to say,
he shares Sidney's distaste [44] for inartistic workmanship which
fails to suit noble words to noble matter. Let anyone who
doubts that the two poets see eye to eye here, read again the
many sallies in *Hamlet, King Lear,* and other plays, on
"words, words, *words,*" and the "*matter*" thereof: "the
phrase would be more germane to the *matter,*" "more *matter*
with less *art,*" "no sallets in the *lines* to make the *matter*

savory, nor no *matter* in the *phrase*," "I love you more than *words* can yield the *matter*." [45]

Nor does Shakespeare deny the force of Sidney's objection to the lack of reasonable propriety in certain of the early plays that pleased the million — his complaint of the want of "decency" and "discretion" in them, whereby "neither . . . commiseration, nor . . . right sportfulness" was "obtained." [46] This is close to the heart of Hamlet's [47] urging that "*discretion* be your tutor," that discretion must ward off such "overdone" or "tardy" action as makes the unskillful laugh and the judicious grieve when the player struts, the poet spices his lines with gross sallets, or the clown, for the benefit of certain barren spectators, speaks more than is set down for him. But these considerations belong more properly to our next subject: Sidney's views on "mongrel tragicomedy," [48] and Shakespeare's practice therein.

Of Tragicomedy

"When Shakespeare," according to Mr. Frank Mathew,[49] "*matched hornpipes with funerals* as the players did when they dissipated the gloom of a tragedy by dancing a jig when it was over, he followed the old ways which were natural to him because he was English." Certain it is that Sidney, like other English critics before him,[50] deprecated what Gascoigne had termed the "indecorum" of "intermingl[ing] merry jests in a serious matter." Some of Sidney's strictures on this subject have been noted above, but a summary of his case against tragicomedy [51] is needed here.

The "gross absurdities" which grew out of the current disregard of the unities of place and time were not the only weak spots. Sidney writes of the contemporary dramatists:

"All their plays be neither right tragedies, nor right comedies; mingling kings and clowns, not because the matter so carrieth it, but thrust in clowns by head and shoulders, to play a part in majestical matters, with neither decency nor discretion: so as neither . . . admiration and commiseration, nor . . . right sportfulness, is by their mongrel tragicomedy obtained." The rare instances of tragicomedy in the work of the ancients — for example, the *Amphitruo* of Plautus — are merely the exceptions which prove the rule. "If we mark them well, we shall find, that they never, or very daintily, *match hornpipes and funerals* . . . . in that comical part of our tragedy," therefore, "we have nothing but scurrility . . . or some extreme show of doltishness . . . where the whole tract of a comedy should be full of delight, as the tragedy should be still maintained in a well raised admiration."

If Sidney had lived on some twenty-five years more, he might have agreed that Shakespeare, in such plays, for example, as *Measure for Measure*, *Cymbeline*, and even *Troilus and Cressida*, achieved something better than mere scurrility and doltishness, in spite of the fact that these plays *are* neither "right tragedy" nor "right comedy." In some respects, certainly, Shakespeare's practice is not far removed from Sidney's doctrine. Such "tragical-historical" pieces, for instance, as *Richard II* and *Richard III*, far from thrusting in "clowns by head and shoulders," have none at all;[52] and in those that have — the "tragical-*comical*-historical" plays of the Falstaff group — the "clowns" stand shoulder-high with the kings. As for the "all-licensed" fool who outjests his master's heart-struck injuries in *King Lear*: Sidney himself might have granted that this fool is there because he belongs, that "the matter carried it." On the other hand, I have already indicated that Shakespeare, no less than Sidney, flinched at the crude mingling of mirth and tragedy in the popular medleys, such as that in the "lamentable tragedy mixed full of pleasant mirth" entitled *King Cambises*,[53] which Falstaff laughed out of court.[54] The first inclination of Duke Theseus in *A Midsummer Night's Dream* (I, ii, 12; V, i, 56–60) was to do just that with "The most Lamentable Comedy and most Cruel Death of Pyramus and Thisby":

> "A tedious brief scene of young Pyramus
> And his love Thisby; very tragical mirth."
> Merry and tragical? tedious and brief?
> That is hot ice and wondrous strange snow.
> How shall we find the concord of this discord?

Of Comedy: definition and function; abuse; right use defended; proper subjects and characters; comic laughter.

As intimated above, Sidney grants freely that "our tragedies and comedies" ["those that I have seen"] are "(not without cause cried out against), observing rules neither of honest civility nor of skillful poetry."[55] Abuse of "the comic" by "naughty play-makers and stage-keepers" has "justly made" it "odious." But "the right use of comedy" has high values. Artistically and ethically they make themselves felt through "the force truth hath in nature," by showing "men play[ing] their parts." For "comedy is an imitation of the common errors of our life . . . represente[d] in the most ridiculous and *scornful* sort that may be"; i.e., in Hamlet's phrase, by "show[ing] *scorn* her own image." "It is impossible," Sidney adds, "that any beholder can be content to be such a one," since "nothing can more open his eyes than to find his own actions contemptibly set forth."

Shakespeare, as might be expected, does not dwell upon

the abstract aspects of these Aristotelian-Sidneyan definitions. He does, however, in Christopher Sly's query,[56] formulate a negative but cogently practical definition of comedy. Sly, the drunken tinker in *The Taming of the Shrew*, wants to know whether "comonty" is not "a Christmas gambold or a tumbling trick?" "No," says the lady, "it is more pleasing stuff. . . . It is a kind of history." In short, the notion that a nonsensical tumbling trick is comedy is a drunken tinker's notion. Almost equally besotted is the small-ale fancy that comedy is no more than a riotous Christmas revel of fools and zanies of the sort which Berowne disparages in *Love's Labour's Lost*,[57] though Sir Toby, Sir Andrew, and Feste in *Twelfth Night* demonstrate that a Christmas revel can play its part in the making of a joyous comedy. Shakespeare, however, does not stop with negative definitions. It was his mind and spirit which poured forth upon our earth the most heart-warming flood of mirth that has yet rolled down the stream of time.[58] That great river keeps rolling along. It does so not least because Shakespeare liked and knew what he was about, knew what enables comedy to achieve its timeless function of giving pleasure to kings and commoners, and what others before him had done in this kind: in "the old comedy,[59] "pleasant comedy," [60] "sweet comedy," [61] in the shaping of "mirthful comic shows/Such as befits the pleasure of the court" [62] and the country.

More specifically, Shakespeare illustrates, time and time again, Sidney's positive claims for comedy, especially its service in holding up the mirror of scorn and ridicule for the self-contemplation of erring mankind. Malvolio and the strutting Ajax, Sir Andrew Aguecheek and Shallow, and many another of their ilk, amply illustrate this fact; and Jaques in *As You Like It* (II, vii, 43–87) unmistakably underscores the principle. His objective, he announces, is to "cleanse the foul body of th' infected world" of pride and folly. He begs the good Duke to invest him speedily in his motley so that he may, in effect, "contemptibly set forth" the follies of wise men and fools, city madams and courtiers, by "anatomizing" them:

> And they that are most galled with my folly,
> They most must laugh.

We must, to be sure, make allowance here for a demurrer by the good Duke, and for a double warning by good Sir Philip: the latter mentions among the objections of the poet-whippers the fact that "they say the comedies rather *teach* than reprehend amorous conceits"; and later, for himself, he "speak[s] to this purpose, that all the end of the comical part be not upon such scornful matters as stirreth laughter only, but, mixed with it . . . delightful teaching. . . . And the great fault even in that point of laughter, and forbidden plainly by Aristotle, is that they stir laughter in sinful things, which are rather execrable than ridiculous." [63] This would seem to be close to that sporting with "crimes" rather than "follies" to which Ben Jonson [64] also objected, and not far from the good Duke's warning to Jaques, against the disgorging of "mischievous foul sin" under the guise of satire. What would he do "but good" with his comic anatomizing, Jaques asks. The Duke answers:

> Most mischievous foul sin, in chiding sin.
> For thou thyself hast been a libertine. . . .
> And all th' embossed sores and headed evils
> That thou with license of free foot hast caught,
> Wouldst thou disgorge into the general world.
> [II, vii, 64–69.]

Perhaps [65] the Duke's charge is not to be taken too seriously. In any case, the real answer to it, that the abuse of comedy does *not* "make" its "right use odious," comes with better grace from the knightly Sidney [66] than from the somewhat weather-beaten Jaques. Yet this very Jaques, "the sundry contemplation" of whose "travels" had wrapped him "in a most humorous sadness," was, according to Sidney's own pronouncement, a proper character for comedy. "A busy loving courtier, a heartless threatening Thraso, a self-wise-seeming schoolmaster, a[n] *awry-transformed traveller*" — "these," Sidney writes,[67] "if we saw walk in stage names . . . therein were delightful laughter." By the same token, it follows that Sidney would have admitted as proper subjects for comic laughter such personages as King Ferdinand and his loving lords in *Love's Labour's Lost*, and their not too wise-seeming schoolmaster Holofernes,[68] together with the loud-mouthed Pistol and the empty threatening Parolles. Who can doubt, moreover, that Sidney, if he had lived to "see" them, would have welcomed with delightful laughter such personages as Mercutio and Dogberry, Benedick and Beatrice, Autolycus and Juliet's nurse?

To conclude this section, it will be worth our while to glance at Sidney's challenging discussion of comic laughter, and Shakespeare's responsive practice. Sidney [69] urges that "loud laughter" is not the be-all and end-all of comedy: "Comedy should be full of delight. . . . But our comedians think there is no delight without laughter; which is very wrong, for though laughter may come with delight, yet cometh it not of delight. . . . Delight hath a joy in it. . . . . Laughter hath only a scornful tickling. . . . We laugh at de-formed creatures, wherein certainly we cannot delight . . . .

the end of . . . [comedy is] not . . . such scornful matters as
stirreth laughter only, but, mixed with it . . . delightful teaching." Yet Sidney does not "deny" that delight and laughter
"may go well together." Now it is certain (as Sidney admits) that laughter need not have "only a scornful tickling."
Witness Touchstone and Bottom the Weaver and Falstaff.
Still, one does not forget Hamlet's objection to the fool's trick
of rousing barren spectators to silly laughter, nor Benedick's
comment upon foolish laughter "at . . . shallow follies." [70]
Christopher Sly's drunken notion of comedy also marks clearly
Shakespeare's agreement with Sidney, as do Berowne and
Rosaline's words in *Love's Labour's Lost*:[71] that comedy is
not "wild laughter,"

> that loose grace
> Which shallow laughing hearers give to fools.

Yet it goes without saying that, as regards comic laughter,
the practice of the creator of Falstaff bettered the theory of
the poet of the *Arcadia*. The reason is obvious. Shakespeare
had incomparably the more hearty "love of laughter," [72] in-
finitely more comic gusto ("with mirth and laughter let old
wrinkles come"),[73] and (like Falstaff) a better rounded and
therefore more philosophic delight in "the world's pleasure
and the increase of laughter." [74]

*Diction: "swelling phrases"; "letter-coursing"; Ciceronian
and Euphuistic prose; the English language.*

After disposing of "this play matter," Sidney devotes a
retrospective paragraph to lyric poetry, a subject more fully
considered in the first and second parts of his treatise.[75] He
then turns [76] to what he calls "the outside of [poesy] . . .
which is words, or (as I may term it) Diction." One of his

preliminary comments deserves immediate notice here, though it touches not only upon diction but also upon one of those "species" of poetry to be reviewed later in this study: "the lyrical kind of Songs and Sonnets." [77] In a famous sonnet of his own, Sidney the poet had pointed the way:

"Fool!" said my muse to me, "look in thy heart, and write."

The critic of the *Defense* drives home the same idea. Many of the sonneteers, he writes, *"if I were a mistress*, would never persuade me they were in love; so coldly they apply fiery speeches, as men that had rather read lovers' writings, and so caught up certain *swelling phrases* [78] . . . than that in truth they feel those passions. . . . So is that honey-flowing Matron Eloquence appareled, or rather disguised, in a courtesan-like, painted affectation." Here I reluctantly interrupt Sir Philip's eloquence to recall several Shakespearean utterances to much the same effect. "If I were a mistress" inevitably brings to mind "My mistress's eyes are nothing like the sun" — even though Sidney and Shakespeare were not the only sonneteers who protested that their loves were not belied with false compare. And Shakespeare, if we may assume that in the long run his characters sometimes speak for him, deprecated empty "swelling phrases" and "courtesan-like, painted affectation" almost as outspokenly as Sidney himself. Shakespeare's utterances on the subject are many and varied. They range all the way from Timon's bitterly ironic praise of the peddler poet whose

> verse *swells* with *stuff so fine* and smooth
> That thou art even natural in thine art,[79]

to Berowne's promise that he will woo in "russet yea's and honest kersey no's," forswearing

> Taffeta phrases, silken terms precise,
> Three-pil'd hyperboles, spruce *affectation*,
> *Figures* pedantical,

those "summer flies" which have "blown" him "full of mag-got ostentation." [80] As for Shakespeare's protests against courtesan-like, painted affectation, I would recall, among others, King Claudius's self-reproachful meditation:

> The *harlot's* cheek, beautied with plast'ring art,
> Is not more ugly to the thing that helps it
> Than is my deed to my most *painted word*.[81]

Sidney's onslaught against the poetic word-mongers goes on apace. They offend "one time" with monstrous "far-fet[ched] words" that "must seem strangers to any poor Englishman" (query: such "fire-new" and "high-born" "golden words" as the fashionable Armado's and the fluttering Osric's?); [82] "another time, with *coursing of a letter*, as if they were bound to follow the method of a dictionary; an-other time, with *figures and flowers*, extremely winter-starved." These are the "*figures* pedantical" which Berowne forswore but the "gifted" Holofernes did not [83] — he who delights in the game of coursing a letter:

> I will something affect the letter, for it argues facility.
> "The preyful princess pierc'd and prick'd a
>   pretty pleasing pricket." [84]

Holofernes never forswears his fine linguistic feathers. Be-rowne does, though his are no goose feathers. Between them, the two admirably illustrate Sidney's ever timely observation: "I have found in diverse smally learned courtiers a more sound style than in some professors of learning." [85]

Even so, "the tongue touches," as the old proverb says,

"where the tooth aches." A glance at *Love's Labour's Lost*, the *Arcadia*, and the *Defense* demonstrates that Shakespeare and Sidney, each in his own way a true son of the Renaissance, merely reprehended the overdoing of the thing they both loved to do: to give "the tongue a helpful ornament," [86] to adorn "that blessing of speech" [87] with all the taffeta phrases, all the fine figures, all the plentiful conceits the matter might "carry." But as good artists they were keenly aware of the obvious fact that a good thing can be carried too far — can be made as tiresome by "ridiculous excess" [88] as the taste of too much sweetness, "whereof a little more than a little is by much too much." [89] Sidney points out that it had been grossly overdone, not only by the "versifiers" but also by the "prose-printers," especially the Ciceronians [90] and the Euphuists. The former "now cast sugar and spice upon every dish that is served to the table"; that is to say, in Shakespeare's words, they will "have honey a sauce to sugar." [91] The latter offend not only with too much wordplay and "letter-coursing" alliteration, relatively venial faults, to judge by the *Arcadia* and *Love's Labour's Lost*, but also with too much unnatural natural history. Sidney complains that "all herbarists, all stories of beasts, fowls and fishes are rifled up . . . they come in [such] multitudes to wait upon . . . our conceits" that the audience cannot but tire of the Euphuists' obvious endeavor "to speak curiously" rather than "truly." [92] This was the passage of the *Defense* which Drayton praised highly a few years after Shakespeare's death, because Sidney it was who

> did first reduce
> Our tongue from Lyly's writing, then in use, —
> Talking of stones, stars, plants, of fishes, flies,
> Playing with words and idle similes.[93]

It goes without saying that Shakespeare would have been aware of the Euphuists even if Sidney had never written, but the chances are that he, like Drayton, saw Sidney's remarks. Certainly he did not scorn to use the fabulous folklore of the Euphuists; for example, Lear's pelican daughters, Edward's pelican son in *Richard II*, [94] and Juliet's — and the good Duke's — loathed toad, jewel-eyed but ugly and venomour.[95] But, like Sidney, he also laughed at their excesses. "There is a thing" called "pitch," says Falstaff, which "as ancient writers do report, doth defile." And there is a plant the like of which was well known to the Euphuistic herbarists: "For though the camomile, the more it is trodden on, the faster it grows, yet youth, the more it is wasted the sooner it wears." [96]

Sidney brings "this wordish consideration," and therewith this part of his treatise, to a fitting close with a short excursus upon the English language.[97] Only two items thereof call for notice here. (1) The first is Sidney's point that our English language, our mother tongue "is particularly happy in compositions of two or three words together . . . which is one of the greatest beauties can be in a language." [98] Professor Cook [99] has shown that Sidney himself loved to use these compounds (for example, "heart-ravishing," "winter-starved"), "not only in prose but in the comparatively sober style of the *Defense*." Romeo's "love-devouring death," *Love's Labour's Lost*'s "honey-tongued Boyet," that "little seeming-substance" Cordelia, and "this bed-presser, this horseback-breaker" Falstaff,[100] are but a few of many examples which might be cited to show that Shakespeare, like many of his fellows, also liked "compositions" in verse and prose. (2) Like a true Elizabethan, and like all the English poets from Chaucer to Masefield, Sidney loved his mother tongue, and loved to praise it. "For the uttering sweetly . . . the conceits of the mind," he wrote,[101] "that hath it equally with any other tongue in the world." Of course Shakespeare did not need Sidney's inspiration — nor did Spenser, Drayton, Samuel Daniel, or Francis Bacon — to teach him the love of England and his mother tongue. This much, however, is clear. He and Sidney were at one in their love of English speech, of "an English ditty," [102] an old English song such as moves the heart more than a trumpet. No "true-born Englishman" of them all loved his "tongue's use," his "native English," the "language" Shakespeare "had learned these forty years," [103] better than did these two.

DEFENSE: PART ONE

Poetry in General: its low estate; divine origin; immortal garlands; relation to verse and rhyme; powers, ethical and artistic.

In this chapter I shall review the main elements of the first part of Sidney's essay [1] and their Shakespearean connotations. At the outset, the motive underlying Sidney's work deserves notice. He undertook his "pitiful defense of poor poetry" because "from almost the highest estimation of learning" it had "fallen to be the laughing-stock of children." [2] "Embraced in all other places," it could "find in our time [only] a hard welcome in England": that "mother of excellent minds" had "grown so hard a step-mother to poets." [3] Yet poetry has ever been "the first light-giver to ignorance, and first nurse." [4] Though it is an art (and therefore, like "the fertilest ground," requires industrious cultivation [5]) it *moves* "with the force of a divine breath," because it is primarily a "divine gift," of "heavenly . . . title." [6] Its civilizing, that is to say its ethical and artistic, powers made it the first and most "profitable" of the arts — for poets "both . . . delight and teach," and thus "*move* men to take . . . goodness in hand." [7] By training men to "find [noble] pleasure" they achieve the true end of "the sweet delights of poetry." For the best "learning is . . . that which teacheth and moveth to virtue, and . . . none can both teach and move thereto so much as poetry." [8] In earliest times "this heart-ravishing knowledge," with its "charming sweetness" [9] enabled the poets "to draw . . . wild untamed wits to an admiration of knowledge" — among them "even . . . the most barbarous and simple Indians." By the same virtue "Amphion was" able "to move stones . . . and Orpheus . . . beasts, indeed stony and beastly people." [10] Those who, while "professing learning, inveigh against poetry," are guilty of ingratitude to their "fathers in learning." They blindly promote "civil war among the Muses." [11] For example, they ignore the fact that neither history nor philosophy "could . . . have entered into the gates of popular judgments, if they had not taken a great passport of poetry." [12] They forget that poetry "doth most polish" the "blessing of speech," and "the just praise it hath" as "the only fit speech for music." [13] And they disregard its claims as the only true exceller of nature (for nature's "world is brazen, the poets only deliver a golden"), and as the only true bestower of immortality ("believe" the poets: "they will make you immortal by their verses"). [14]

The views just summarized flow in the main current of Renaissance criticism,[15] but their affirmative emphasis, their noble eloquence of faith and phrase, is Sidney's own. If, therefore, Shakespeare read the *Defense* at all, it seems likely that he would have noticed — and not improbable that he might have remembered — some of these eloquent passages. This is not to say that Sidney was Shakespeare's only source of information on the questions involved, or to deny that some of the likenesses between the two poets may be commonplaces. Sidney and Shakespeare, for example, were not the only Elizabethans who wrote of the miserable state into which poor poetry had fallen. Shakespeare alludes to the sub-

ject in the "satire keen and critical" proposed for the enter-
tainment of the court in *A Midsummer Night's Dream*:

> "The thrice three Muses mourning for the death
> Of Learning, late deceas'd in beggary";
>
> (V, i, 52–54)

but Spenser [16] had repeatedly used this theme before Shakespeare, and it frequently reappeared, later, in the writings of
such poets as Dekker, Daniel, Ben Jonson, and Milton.[17] It
must also be granted at once that Shakespeare did not neces-
sarily remember Sidney only when, like him, he hailed "sweet
poetry," [18] paid tribute to its dream of "the golden world," [19]
proclaimed anew the familiar doctrine of its divine origin
("Much is the force of heaven-bred poesy"),[20] reëmphasized
the close relationship between music and poetry,[21] and re-
asserted its primary claims as the true bestower of immortal
garlands:

> Not marble nor the gilded monuments
> Of princes shall outlive this pow'rful rhyme.[22]

More significant, in my judgment, is the frequently recurring Shakespearean reëmphasis, in thought and phrase, of
other familiar ideas upon which Sidney loved to dwell. I
refer especially to his concern for the ethical-aesthetic function: "that delightful teaching which is the end of poesy." [23]
We have seen the sterner implications of this doctrine in
Hamlet's observation that the purpose of playing is to show
virtue her own feature, scorn her own image. In serener
moods Shakespeare re-echoes other favorite Platonic-Hora-
tian principles of Sidney's, particularly the belief that "virtue
no delighted *beauty* lack[s],[24] that "*virtue* and true
beauty" [25] go together, and that "*delight* writ . . . with

beauty's pen" [26] is essential to the process whereby, as Berowne intimates, "that angel knowledge" can conquer "bar-
barism" and poetry can humanize learning.[27] "O what
learning is!" sighs Juliet's nurse, and old Gremio, in *The
Taming of the Shrew*, echoes the sentiment with all his
heart: "This learning, what a thing it is!" [28] The nurse
could have sat up half the night to listen to the learned friar
— and no wonder! Who could not, if this thing "which
commonly we call learning" be indeed such a "purifying of
wit . . . enriching of memory . . . enlarging of conceit" as
Sidney postulates [29] and Shakespeare dramatizes (especially in
Love's Labour's Lost, where matchless Navarre and his spir-
ited bookmen disport themselves in their pleasant Academe,
and in *The Taming of the Shrew*, when Lucentio goes to
seek out "a course of learning and ingenious study" in fair
Padua). What they seek is not the "lean and wasteful learning" [30] of the schools. They abjure painful pedantry, which
pores

> upon a book
> To seek the light of truth while truth the while
> Doth falsely blind the eyesight of his look . . .
> Study is like the heaven's glorious sun. . . .
> Small have continual plodders ever won
> Save base authority from others' books.[31]

What they do want is clearly implied in another remark of
Berowne's:

> Learning is but *an adjunct to ourself*,
> And where we are our learning likewise is.[32]

"Study's god-like recompense," [33] in short, is learning humanized: quickened by the sweet delights of youth and
love and poetry. The principle is stated unmistakably by

Tranio in *The Taming of the Shrew* (I, i, 28–40), when he applauds his master's resolution "to suck the sweets of sweet philosophy," but makes the point that "profitable" learning must have a rational basis of humane pleasure:

> Let's be no Stoics nor no stocks, I pray. . . .
> Balk logic with acquaintance that you have,
> And practice rhetoric in your common talk;
> Music and poesy use to quicken you. . . .
> No profit grows where is no pleasure taken.

Sidney and Shakespeare are agreed that it is this impassioned learning, this "heart-ravishing" knowledge which gives poetry its civilizing power. Lorenzo in *The Merchant of Venice* says,[34]

> Therefore the poet
> Did feign that Orpheus drew trees, stones and floods;

therefore, in Berowne's words, the poet's pen can "ravish savage ears," even the "rude and savage man of Inde." [35]

Vigorously and often our poets emphasize a closely related principle. True poetry, they hold, is a quickening power, an essential virtue, not to be mistaken for what may be merely its limbs and outward flourishes. External form does not make poetry. "Poets," Sidney writes,[36] "*apparel* . . . their poetical inventions in that numbrous kind of writing which is called verse: indeed but *apparel* . . . verse being but an ornament and no cause to poetry, since there have been many most excellent poets that never versified, and now swarm many versifiers that need never answer to the name of poets." Although, as he adds, later, he would be the last "to scorn the sacred mysteries of poesy," or "to jest at the reverent title of a rimer," his purpose is clear: "I speak to show that it is not riming and versing that maketh a poet, no more than a long gown maketh an advocate." "One may be a poet without versing, and a versifier without poetry."

Anyone who knows Shakespeare, knows that he is equally outspoken on this subject. "Scald rhymers," "metre ballad-mongers," "fellows of infinite tongue that can rhyme themselves into ladies' favours" (i.e., cheap poetasters "versing love" in "*bad*" verses" [37]) get short shrift from Shakespeare or from some of his liveliest characters.[38] King Henry V says flatly that "a rhyme is but a ballad," and Benedick's idea of a prize indignity is to have one's eyes picked out with a ballad-maker's pen.[39] Accordingly, poor Orlando, love-lorn in Arden, does not fare too well when his lame-foot verses stumble into the presence of his much berhymed but unbemused Rosalind, especially after running the gauntlet of Touchstone's even more impartial judgment: "I'll rhyme you so eight years together. . . . It is the right butter-women's rank to market . . . . the very false gallop of verses." [40] In short, with a moderate shift in emphasis one might almost say that Hotspur speaks for Shakespeare when he remarks that nothing sets his teeth on edge so much as "*mincing* poetry." [41] Mere "riming and versing" Sidney called it: verses that sound in Hotspur's ears "like the forced gait of a shuffling nag"; "vile" rhymes, "rude, harsh-sounding" or "babbling" rhymes, with "neither rhyme nor reason" to recommend them.[42] Even so, every page of the plays makes certain the fact that Shakespeare, like Sidney, loved "true" rhymes; "true," "gracious," and "fiery numbers"; and "happy verse" — "brave," "magic verses." [43]

Sidney's eloquent prose testifies to the same purpose. In spite of the rhymesters and verse mongers, "indeed the Senate

of Poets hath chosen verse as their fittest raiment . . . not
.speaking (table talk fashion or like men in a dream) words as
they chanceably fall from the mouth, but peising each syllable
of each word by just proportion [a phrase which Shakespeare
also used] [44] according to the dignity of the subject." Verse,
Sidney later says, "doth most polish that blessing of speech,"
and also, by fostering measured harmony, makes poetry "the
only fit speech for music." [45] Then too, poetry can accom-
plish the "knitting up of the memory" far better than can prose.
By way of proving this last point, Sidney cites an instance
duly verified by Shakespeare. In Sidney's words: "What
needeth more in a thing so known to all men? Who is it
that ever was a scholar that doth not carry away some verses
of Virgil, Horace, of Cato, which in his youth he learned?" [46]
Shakespeare's verification appears in *Titus Andronicus*: [47]

> O, 'tis a verse in Horace. I know it well.
> I read it in the grammar long ago.

All this implies that Shakespeare and Sidney agreed upon
a basic principle which Ben Jonson also underscored when
he praised Shakespeare's art:

> Yet must I not give nature all; thy art,
> My gentle Shakespeare, must enjoy a part.

"A poet no industry can make," Sidney had written,[48] "if
his own genius be not carried into it. . . . Yet as the fertilest
ground must be manured" so must the poet's genius be de-
veloped by "art, imitation, and exercise." Though I have
touched elsewhere [49] upon Shakespeare's general reaction to
this principle, the essential elements of his position must be
noticed here. He knew, for example, that on occasion art
might be "tongue-tied by authority," [50] but he recognized

the artist's obligation to take pains, in spite of the world, the
flesh, and the devil. True poetry, he suggests, by way of
ironic commentary upon Timon's peddler poet, is not "a
thing slipped idly" from the artist's brain and heart: "our
poesy" is not "a gum which oozes/From whence 'tis nour-
ished." [51] Hamlet is "ill at these numbers," because he had
"not art," time, or patience to make them good.[52] Benedick
tries his hand, however haltingly, at verses "truly turned over
and over," and his laborious effort is not without reward. It
teaches him, in spite of his jesting, to value the inspired art of
the true poems — the old tales of Leander, and Troilus, and
all the rest "whose names yet run smoothly in the even road
of a blank verse." [53] Sidney,[54] once more, observed that after
Chaucer other English poets, "encouraged and delighted" by
his "excellent" art, "followed to *beautify our mother tongue.*"
Shakespeare's Glendower is a Welshman, but that fact does
not prevent him from claiming the same virtue for his English poetry (*1 Henry IV*, III, i, 121–125). He says to
Hotspur:

> I can speak *English*, lord, as well as you;
> For I was train'd up in the English court,
> Where, being but young, I framed to the harp
> Many an English ditty lovely well
> *And gave the tongue a helpful ornament.*

Glendower and the English poets achieved their end by
the same means. Their art — for example, that "exquisite
observing of number and measure in words" which Sidney [55]
praised — made good their inspiration. "Marry, they that
delight in poesy . . . should seek to know what they do, and
how they do." The proper formula for them, Sidney suggests, is painstaking "industry" plus "genius." Only those

whose work combines these two essentials can achieve what even Holofernes the pedant recognized as "the elegancy, facility, and golden cadence of poesy." [56]

Poetry and the Creative Imagination

Fundamental in the *Defense* is Sidney's insistence upon the importance of the creative imagination. "High flying liberty of conceit" is not merely "proper to the poet," it is essential. The poet, "lifted up with the vigor of his own invention," and "disdaining to be tied" to the "subjection" of literal fact, "doth grow in effect another nature . . . making things either better than nature [57] . . . or quite anew." [58] Shakespeare's Duke Theseus, in the great passage upon which I have drawn earlier in this study,[59] agrees in principle, albeit with some reluctance — since "cool reason" must needs wonder whether unchecked imaginings may not produce mere "fantasies" "more strange than true." By and large, however, Theseus, like Sir Philip, acclaims the vast power and range of the poetic imagination: the mighty sweep from heaven to earth which bodies forth and names forever more the forms of things unknown, even such "airy nothings" as "never were." [60] Sidney the Platonist, however, soars into still higher regions — into the heaven of heavens. Indeed, he does not deem it "too saucy a comparison" to liken the creative virtue of the true poet or "maker" to that of "the heavenly Maker of that maker." For the most excellent "skill" of the great Artificer, according to Sidney,[61] "standeth in" the "*fore-conceit* of the work, and not in the work itself." And this holds true of the poet's creations. His works, "deliver[ed] forth in such excellency as he hath imagined them . . . when with the force of a divine breath he bringeth things forth far surpassing her [Nature's] doings," manifest the all but divine [62] virtue of *the poet's* "fore-conceit." Sidney adds that few may grant these arguments, but at least one element of his comparison between the heavenly Maker and the earthly is implicit in another great passage of Shakespeare's. In Prospero's vision Shakespeare poignantly recognizes the limitations of our mortality. But, in so doing, he likens the mutable creation of the artist-sage to that of the heavenly Maker. "We are such stuff as dreams are made on"; our best work, the fabric of the greatest poet's vision, is insubstantial, must fade — but *so shall God's great globe itself*:

> Yea, all which it inherit, shall dissolve,
> And, like this insubstantial pageant faded,
> Leave not a rack behind.[63]

The solemn undertones of Prospero's verses bear another burden, less distinctly audible in the youthful music of *A Midsummer Night's Dream*. *The Tempest* reveals something of the mind and heart of a poet who lived to be older and greater than Sidney, nor can one study this play without realizing that the concept of the creative imagination in Shakespeare's maturer works was not bounded by his predecessor's. Though many significant utterances of Shakespeare's on this subject are close to Sidney's, others point toward certain differences between the two poets. For example: Shakespeare, in one sense, had more faith than Sidney in the efficacy of the imagination, a greater faith which enabled him to overleap the other's critical inhibitions.[64] In fairness to Sidney, however, it should be noted at once that at least one passage in the *Defense* cogently anticipates one of Shakespeare's best answers to Sidney's objections. The passage appears in Sidney's refutation of the charge that poets lie. The truth is, says Sidney, that the poet does not pretend to present literal reality, and does not expect his work to be accepted as such. "The poet . . . never affirmeth. . . . never maketh any circles about your imagination, to conjure you to believe for true what he writes. . . . What child is there that, coming to a play, and seeing Thebes written in great letters upon an old door, doth believe that it is Thebes?" [65] We have already observed [66] that Shakespeare, for his part, triumphantly demonstrates — in *Henry V* and *The Winter's Tale* — his reliance upon the audience's "imaginary puissance" as a sufficient means to achieve the poet's ends without subservient adherence to the unities, with an eye to the "liberty" rather than to "the law of writ." But Shakespeare's faith in the imagination, though fortified by mighty works, was ever vulnerable, never altogether secure against persistent self-questioning. The *Defense* by and large manifests an eloquently unqualified, almost an ecstatic, faith in the all-sufficiency of the imagination's creative virtue. Theseus' observations concerning the lunatic, the lover, and the poet suggest that Sidney's eloquence left its mark upon Shakespeare's memory. But one does not forget Puck's epilogue — "If we shadows have offended" — and Mercutio's remarks on "vain fantasy," [67] nor the deeper cadences of Prospero's meditation, and the great sonnets on time and change. These sufficiently illustrate Shakespeare's sober second thoughts: his tendency to balance the exuberant claims of "strong imagination" with a brooding awareness of the impermanence of beauty and of the shadowy insubstantiality of art. Sidney, for his part, was too true an artist to be blind to these darker realities of the poet's vision, but he rarely dwells upon them, either in the *Defense* or in his sonnets.[68] His admission that "the poet's persons and doings *are but pictures*" is notable because it anticipates in a measure Theseus' remark to Hippolyta, "the best in this kind *are but shadows*.[69] But Sidney's remark is the exception which in his case proves the rule. It is Shakespeare rather than Sidney who tends to question, now and again, the very virtue he exalts. One of Shakespeare's characters in the second part of *Henry IV*,[70] for example, virtually repeats Theseus' observation that imagination is as "proper to madmen" as to poets. And it is Shakespeare's critical observation — not Sidney's — that imagination per se may "jade" [71] as well as inspire; that there is "salt imagination" [72] as well as sweet, "wrong imagination" [73] as well as right; that "imaginary work" may be "deceitful," [74] may transform "a bush" into "a bear," [75] may become, at worst, a hollow lure for "fools," [76] and at best, sometimes, an inadequate substitute for reality:

> O, who can hold a fire in his hand
> By thinking on the frosty Caucasus?
> Or cloy the hungry edge of appetite
> By bare imagination of a feast?
> Or wallow naked in December snow
> By thinking on fantastic summer's heat? [77]

Perhaps it was because Shakespeare kept his feet firmly on solid ground that his eyes were able to see most clearly, to glance most keenly, most comprehensively, from earth to heaven. Certain it is that he knew not only the rush and splendor of creation but also many a questioning mood, many an endeavor to measure the immeasurable, to compass his own flights, to scrutinize curiously what seemed to him the all too shadowy texture of even the mightiest poet's dream.

And yet, in spite of "cool reason" and persistent self-questioning, he was scarcely second even to Sidney in paying tribute to the overplus of virtue in this supreme gift of all true poets: "big" imagination, "great" imagination, "strong" imagination, "shaping" imagination.[78]

Sidney and Shakespeare also reached substantial agreement upon two corollaries to this proposition: both champion the poetic imagination against the age-old but ever new attacks of puritanical or literal minded objectors, and both delight in the special power by which it wins some of its greatest victories: its gift of story-telling.

Francis Bacon recalled in his essay "Of Truth" that "one of the fathers, in great severity" condemned "poesy . . . because it filleth the imagination . . . with the shadow of a lie." Sidney's answer — his eloquent refutation of the ancient libel against poetry, or, more particularly, against the poetic imagination, as "the mother of lies" — is the main theme of the second part of the *Defense*. That answer, therefore, together with Shakespeare's allusions to the subject, will be reviewed in the concluding part of this study. For the moment we have still to notice that Sidney and Shakespeare deal with another complaint of the enemies of the poetic imagination, those who charged it with being not only "falsely" inspired but "fantastically" misdirected,[79] that is to say, not only with untruth but with unreality. Against these literalists both our poets, and Sidney in particular, spoke out in unmistakable terms. The poet-haters belittled the make-believe, the "fiction" of poetry; they reprehended its supposedly unreal "feigning." [80] As a matter of fact, this creative imagining, this bodying forth, in Shakespeare's phrase, of "all that poets feign of bliss and joy," [81] this revelation of truth soaring heaven-high above the dull mists of casual matter-of-fact which Sidney calls the "bare *Was*" of history,[82] this, according to the *Defense*, is poetry's special glory. Even at their lowest level, the poet's imaginings may be at least as valid as merely factual occurrences: in a given case "Xenophon's fiction" serves at least as useful a purpose as Livy's "verity," and in other instances the poet's "feigned examples" are "so much the better," so "certainly . . . more doctrinable," as the "feigned Aeneas in Virgil" is better than "the right Aeneas in Dares Phrigius."[83] All this because the feigned example, "tuned to the highest key of passion," is fitter "both for further teaching, and more delighting."[84] This, then, is the true touchstone of poetry. "Not riming and versing . . . maketh a poet" but the creative imagination: "that feigning" of "notable images of virtues, vices, or what else with . . . delightful teaching . . . must be the right describing note to know a poet by."[85] And this is also the essential note of Shakespeare's faith. As usual with him, it is not an unquestioning faith, for he was never unaware of that sort of feigning which is not imaginative creation but merely the pretentious or false display of cheap poetasters such as Timon's, or of "feigned friends," "feigned prayer," and "feigned ecstasies."[86] But for Shakespeare too the right describing note, however lightly or seriously sounded by Theseus, Viola, Olivia, or Touchstone, is an assertion of faith in that true feigning which is the essence of poetry. For him, almost as truly as for Wordsworth, it is imagination which bodies forth not only "the forms of things unknown" but "the consecration and the poet's dream" — the "thoughts beyond the reaches of our souls." The more truly "poetical" a thing is, "the more like" it is "to be feigned."[87] The most truly

inspired poetry, according to Touchstone, is the most imaginative: "truest poetry is the most feigning." [88] In other
words, it is "of imagination all compact." And this sort of
poetry is most likely to be achieved by the "good fellow poet"
to whom the gods have given the special grace which moves
all human hearts.

I have previously given two notable instances of Shakespeare's hearty agreement with Sidney's principle that the
poet's imagination achieves its happiest effects when it holds
children from play and old men from the chimney corner by
eloquent story-telling, such as made aged and younger ears
play truant when Berowne was in the vein or Menenius
told his pretty tale of the belly and the body's mutinous members. In every mood, everywhere and always, Shakespeare
demonstrated by his works his adherence to this basic tenet
of the faith. Almost every page of his is a poem full of
stories: "twice-told" tales of ages long ago, merry or sad, of
sorrow or of joy; "tedious" tales and "sensible" tales and
"pretty" tales — the story of the Prodigal and the tale of
Philomel — and tales whose lightest word would harrow up
our souls; stories "shallow" or "deep" written "in love's
richest book," of young Leander and true Romeo and proud
Cleopatra; sad stories of the deaths of kings, a tale told by
an idiot, a woman's story by a winter's fire, and a round
unvarnished tale such as won the gentle Desdemona.

"Parts, Kinds, or Species" of Poetry

In the same paragraph of the *Defense* which urges that
"feigning" of notable images of virtues and vices is the
essence of poetry, Sidney enumerates its "sundry . . . special [89] denominations"; i.e., its "parts, kinds, or species":

"the heroic, lyric, tragic, comic, satiric, iambic, elegiac, pastoral, and certain others" [90] — including the "mingled" kinds later identified as the "tragi-comical," the "mingled . . . heroical and pastoral," etc.[91] In point of fact, the actual discussion of these several species of poetry is made to wait upon an important digression. Sidney proceeds to examine the claims of history and philosophy, "the principal challengers" of "the poet's nobleness" — and concludes that the poet far excels these competitors: is, indeed, "prince . . . over all the rest" of the arts because he is "the most excellent workman," the prime mover to "virtuous action." [92] For our purposes, history and philosophy must wait their turn till we have reviewed what Sidney and Shakespeare say about poetry's parts and kinds. Several general considerations, however, deserve preliminary notice.

First: Since this part of our study turns about points of more or less formal analysis, we shall hardly expect the casual utterances of Shakespeare the dramatist to match closely or balance nicely the considered findings of Sidney the critic. Still, in view of what has gone before, perhaps it would not be altogether surprising to find Shakespeare, once more, illustrating the principles set up by his predecessor. And possibly — since proof positive is not to be expected — we may find him remembering certain particular details of Sidney's phrasing or approach, such as Polonius' enumeration, already referred to,[93] of the "mingled" dramatic, "tragical-comical-historical-pastoral," kinds. Next, it is to be noted that Sidney's analysis of the parts or species of poetry is relatively brief (he proposes *"in a word* to cite the special kinds"), eclectic ("perchance forgetting some, and leaving some as needless to be remembered"), and aggressively defensive ("to see what faults" — he really means what virtues, what faults if any — "may be found in the right use of them").[94] I have previously discussed the Shakespearean connotations of Sidney's criticism of the dramatic species — tragedy, comedy, and tragicomedy.[95] Here we shall see that Shakespeare does not neglect any of the six non-dramatic kinds enumerated by Sidney, though he does not specifically name three of them: the iambic, the lyric, and the heroical. I shall examine these six non-dramatic species of poetry in the actual sequence of Sidney's own discussion, which begins with a query concerning the pastoral.

1. *The Pastoral.* "Is the poor pipe disdained," which sometimes shows "the misery of people under hard lords or ravening soldiers. . . . sometimes, under the pretty tales of wolves and sheep . . . include[s] the whole considerations of wrong-doing and *patience*," and sometimes demonstrates "that contention for trifles can get but a trifling victory," that quiet "*blessedness* is derived to them that *lie lowest*?" [96] I shall not attempt to repeat here what Professor Greenlaw has admirably said in his general study of Shakespeare's pastorals.[97] Instead, let me recall Menenius' "pretty tale" of the body's members rebelling against the stomach,[98] though it is true enough that neither this nor any of Lucio's "pretty tales" in *Measure for Measure* [99] exemplifies the pretty pastoral "allegories . . . formal tales of beasts" [100] which Sidney had specifically in mind. Shakespeare, in short, wrote no *Shepherd's Calendar* and no *Mother Hubbard's Tale.* Yet his plays do exemplify all the varieties of the pastoral in Polonius' list — "pastoral, pastoral-comical, historical-pastoral . . . tragical-comical-historical-pastoral" [101] — and most of Sidney's pastoral desiderata to boot. For example, at the risk of taking Polonius too seriously, let us recall (1) the

relatively unmingled felicities of the "Whitsun pastorals" in
The Winter's Tale; [102] (2) the pastoral-comical meditations
of the good Duke, and the pleasing pains of Touchstone and
Rosalind and her Orlando in the forest of Arden; [103] (3)
the historical-pastoral touches in *Henry VI* (Parts 2 and
3), [104] *2 Henry IV*, [105] and *Henry V*; [106] and (4) the tragical-comical-historical-pastoral interlude in the mountain
fastnesses of *Cymbeline*'s Wales. [107] Certainly Shakespeare
did not altogether disdain the "poor pipe." He makes it sing
lustily even in so courtly a comedy as *Love's Labour's
Lost*, [108] where "shepherds pipe on oaten straw" at the last.
In sundry places, moreover, he makes the pipe sound Sir
Philip's own notes. Such are the good Duke's "consideration
of wrong-doing and patience" ("Sweet are the uses of adversity") in Arden, and King Henry IV's reiteration of
Sidney's praise of the simple life — the quiet "blessedness"
of those "that *lie lowest*":

> Then happy *low, lie down*!
> Uneasy lies the head that wears a crown. [109]

Such also is the hapless King Henry VI's commentary, on
contentious striving for "trifling victory" and "the misery of
people under hard lords and ravening soldiers," when he be-
holds the bloody horrors of outrageous civil war:

> O, pity, God, this miserable age!
>
> O, pity, pity, gentle heaven, pity!
> The red rose and the white are on his face,
> The fatal colours of our striving houses.
>
> Gives not the hawthorn bush a sweeter shade
> To shepherds looking on their silly sheep
> Than doth a rich embroider'd canopy
> To kings that fear their subjects' treachery? [110]

2. *The Elegiac.* Like the queen in *Richard III*,[111] neither of our poets was "barren to bring forth complaints," but both contented themselves with relatively brief comment on this species: Sidney's "lamenting elegiac" and Shakespeare's "dire-lamenting elegies." [112] Sidney defends the elegiac, within limits. "In a kind heart," he writes, it "would move rather pity than blame," because it "bewails . . . the weakness of mankind and the wretchedness of the world." In fact, it deserves praise for two reasons, not only for its "compassionate" treatment of "just causes of lamentation," but "for rightly painting out how weak be the passions of woefulness." Shakespeare, of course, dramatized over and over again both of these elegiac functions. Romeo's friar, King Claudius in *Hamlet*, and many another Shakespearean king and commoner agree with Sidney that it is natural and "commendable" [113] to lament just causes of grief. But Sidney holds no brief for the sort of "elegy" wherein the poet merely "weeps the want of his mistress." [114] Shakespeare genially lets Orlando hang "odes upon hawthorn and elegies upon brambles," [115] but Shakespeare, too, has little fondness for mere "lamenting toys." [116] Over and over again he suggests that "moderate lamentation" [117] is the right principle: "Why should calamity be full of words?" [118] "Let reason govern thy lament." [119] By the same token, he insinuates a weak falsetto into the "woeful . . . woeful" wailing of the Capulet chorus at the supposed death of Juliet,[120] and shows, in no uncertain terms, how weak is the passion of woefulness when Constance demonstrates that she is as fond of grief as of her child, and Richard II, refusing to resign as King of griefs, plays the wanton with his woes.[121]

3–4. *The Iambic and the Satiric* (i.e., satirical iambics and other poetic forms of satire). Poetic satire, says Sidney, deserves not "mislike" but praise: "the bitter but wholesome iambic" because it "rubs the *galled* mind," making "shame the trumpet of villainy with bold and open crying out against naughtiness," and satirical verse in general because it "never leaveth" until it makes "a man laugh at folly, and, at length ashamed, to laugh at himself." [122] Shakespeare nowhere mentions "the iambic" as such. Yet it is altogether likely that he knew something of it, for Hamlet almost certainly did. One recalls that the Prince of Denmark knew how to make "the *galled* jade wince," and that he poked fun at Polonius *by the book* — that is to say, with "words, words, words," (from one or another satirical or epigrammatic-satirical collection of *Springes to Catch Woodcocks?*) in which "the satirical rogue" said "that old men have grey beards." [123] At all events, Shakespeare knew the ways of what he calls "satire keen and critical," [124] and its function, according to Sidney, of making men "laugh at folly." Jaques says so, in so many words, when he asks the Duke's permission to don the motley:

> And they that are most *galled* with my *folly,*
> They most must laugh . . .
> Give me leave
> To speak my mind, and I will through and through
> Cleanse the foul body of th' infected world.[125]

5. *The Lyric.* This species, says Sidney, is praiseworthy because "his [its] tuned lyre, and well accorded voice, *giveth praise,* the reward of virtue, to virtuous acts . . . [and] sometimes raiseth up his voice to the height of the heavens, in singing the lauds of the immortal God." Then

comes the famous passage concerning the old song of Percy and Douglas, which though "sung but by some blind crowder, with no rougher voice than rude style," Sidney could never hear without finding his "heart moved more than with a trumpet." He admits, however, that such "soldier-like" songs, "chiefest kindlers of brave courage . . . . fit to awake" men from "idleness, to embrace honorable enterprises," were not the only lyrics known in his time: "*They* say the lyric is larded with passionate sonnets." He himself says: "That lyrical kind of *songs and sonnets* . . . how well it might be employed, and with how heavenly fruit . . . in singing the praises of the immortal beauty, the immortal goodness of . . . God." [126] In short, the poet of *Astrophel and Stella*, though not without sins of his own — certain sonnets which, "If I were a mistress, would never persuade me" — [127] was thinking also of "Leave me, O love which reachest but to dust." So Shakespeare, in his plays and sonnets. Slender, in *The Merry Wives*,[128] like Sidney, was fond of his (i.e., Tottel's) "Book of *Songs and Sonnets*." And Shakespeare, like Sidney, protested a little loudly that his mistress' eyes were nothing like the sun. But, again like Sidney, he also addressed an occasional sonnet not to a dark lady but to his "poor soul, the centre of my sinful earth." The word "lyric," incidentally, is not to be found in Shakespeare's pages, but the thing is everywhere, often in terms close to Sidney's. For example: Shakespeare, too, could smile objectively at "passionate" and "wailful sonnets" [129] and all their family of sighs. It is the magnificent Armado who implores Moth: "Warble, child, make passionate my . . . hearing," [130] and it is Shakespeare's conventional lover, sighing like a furnace, who croons woeful ballads made to his mistress' eyebrow.[131] Again, even though "the blind harper's song" mentioned by

Berowne [132] may not be first cousin to the *blind crowder's song* of Percy and Douglas, there can be no mistaking the fact that Shakespeare's heart, too, was moved more than with a trumpet by the power of "old and antique song":

> Come, the song we had last night.
> Mark it, Cesario; it is old and plain.
> The spinsters and the knitters in the sun,
> And the free maids that weave their thread with bones,
> Do use to chant it. It is silly sooth,
> And dallies with the innocence of love,
> Like the old age.[133]

6. *The Heroical.* "There rests," so Sidney concludes, "the heroical . . . which is not only a kind, but the best and most accomplished kind of poetry," because it "teacheth and moveth to the most high and excellent truth." By way of proof he cites an outstanding illustration: "Only let *Aeneas* be *worn in the tablet of your memory* . . . how in storms . . . in war . . . in peace . . . he will be found in excellency fruitful." [134] The heroical, like the lyric, does not appear by name in Shakespeare, but it, too, is everywhere implicit in his pages. Many scores of allusions to old Priam, Anchises, Aeneas, Dido, and the rest appear in his plays, not only in *Troilus* and *Titus* and *Hamlet,* but also in *Julius Caesar, Romeo and Juliet, Antony and Cleopatra,* and elsewhere. One example will suffice, because it proves that Shakespeare, too, wore Aeneas in the tablet of his memory. "One speech," says Hamlet, "I chiefly lov'd. 'Twas *Aeneas'* tale to Dido. . . . *If it live in your memory,* begin . . ." [135]

Poetry's "Challengers": Philosophy and History

Shakespeare never wrote a formal treatise in defense of poetry. Naturally, therefore, he elaborated no comparative analysis of poetry, philosophy, and history as rival claimants to the honor of best achieving Sidney's ideal: "The ending end of all earthly learning . . . virtuous action." [136] Nevertheless, "study," "learning," and "philosophy," as already indicated,[137] do not go without mention in the plays, nor do history and the "good old chronicle[s]." [138] I shall follow Sidney in summarizing: first, the claims of the philosophers, according to his judgment and Shakespeare's.

1. *Philosophy.* "As principal challengers," Sir Philip writes,[139] "step forth the moral philosophers." They approach the eloquent defender of poetry "with a sullen gravity, as though they could not abide vice by daylight" — almost, I am tempted to suggest, like the grave Chief Justice approaching, and reproaching, the young man named Falstaff. At any rate, that "reverent vice, that grey iniquity" tries to pass for one of those

> young men, whom Aristotle thought
> Unfit to hear moral philosophy.

Witness his response to the moral philosopher:

Chief Justice: There is not a white hair on your face but should have his effect of gravity.
Falstaff: His effect of gravy, gravy, gravy.

A moment later, when Falstaff humbly suggests that the Judge lend him a thousand pounds, the other replies: "Not a penny, not a penny." [140] Sidney's philosophers, unlike the closefisted Chief Justice, "cast . . . largess as they go" — albeit largess only of "definitions, divisions, and distinctions." Now "the question is, whether the feigned image of poesy or the regular instruction of philosophy hath the more force in teaching." The answer is that the philosophers are no match for the poet. For they teach "virtue [only] by certain abstract considerations": "obscurely, so as the learned only can understand . . . that are already taught." In short, they make "a school-art of that which the poet . . ." ["the food for the tenderest stomachs . . . the right popular philosopher"] "did only teach by a divine delightfulness." The point would seem to be that the philosophers' learning is that lean and wasteful learning of the schools which Rosalind and Berowne [141] relished no more than did Sir Philip Sidney. Or, for that matter, no more than Romeo, and Hero's father, relished abstract philosophic counsel in the face of their frustrated hope and angry grief:

> Hang up philosophy!
> Unless philosophy can make a Juliet.

> Was never yet philosopher
> That could endure the toothache patiently.[142]

So far as philosophy's teaching is concerned, Sidney reiterates, the trouble is that because "the philosophers . . . scorn to delight, so must they be content little to *move*." For this reason, "Plato and Boethius . . . made Mistress Philosophy very often borrow the masking raiment of poetry" — presumably, to attain what Shakespeare repeatedly described as "the gentle spirit of *moving* words," and "the concord of sweet sound." [143] At all events, in concluding his case against the philosophers, Sidney points out that the current "objections" to the abuse of poetry [144] may justly be "requited" with at least equally valid exceptions "against philosophers"; in other words, against the abuse of philosophy. A similar proposition appears in *Timon of Athens* [145] where it is suggested that the philosophers' charge that poets lie can be turned back against the philosophers:

> *Poet*: How now, philosopher?
> *Apemantus*: Thou liest.
> *Poet*: Art not one?
> *Apemantus*: Yes.
> *Poet*: Then I lie not.

Yet it goes without saying that Sidney and Shakespeare were no enemies to philosophy. Neither of them shared Milton's unqualified delight in it:

> How charming is divine Philosophy!
> Not harsh and crabbed, as dull fools suppose,
> But musical as is Apollo's lute,[146]

but both paid honor where honor is due. Ignorance, according to Shakespeare, is "the curse of God, knowledge the wing wherewith we fly to heaven." [147] Therefore his young men in *Love's Labour's Lost* and *The Taming of the Shrew* — not to mention his stoic old Romans, and young Hamlet at Wittenberg — woo "that angel, knowledge" and "suck the sweets of sweet philosophy" to their hearts' content. It must be said, however, that hardly any one of them is ever quite satisfied with philosophy as an end in itself. *Love's Labour's Lost* makes this abundantly clear. It emphasizes the point that "study's godlike recompense" — the true reward of that angel, knowledge — is a glorious thing; but philosophical pedantry ("painful study") "evermore is overshot." In other words, "living in philosophy" in the narrow sense is a "barren task," "too hard" for young blood and eager hearts. Sidney, with similar reservations, paid reverent tribute to Plato and to many another philosopher. "I honor philosophical instructions," he wrote, "and bless the wits which bred them: so as they be not abused." [148]

2. *History*. Shakespeare had "read in the chronicles";

he says so, in Fluellen's words,[149] and his historical plays
prove it. By and large, Shakespeare probably drew his own
conclusions on the subject of history. Not a few of them,
however, are interesting not only in themselves but because,
for one reason or another, they are close to Sidney's. So far
as Shakespeare's histories are concerned, the fact, once more,
would seem to be that "what Sidney outlined . . . Shakespeare executed." Both of them certainly exalted the poet's
power to "delight" and to "move," above his two challengers'. Sidney puts poesy's "underling historiography"
lower in the scale than philosophy; and we shall find that
Shakespeare, in practice if not in precept, upholds Sidney's
contention that the poet "excelleth history," that "the best
of the historian is subject to the poet," [150] who is, in turn —
as has been shown — superior to the philosopher. But this
does not mean that both men ignore altogether "the *praise*
of history." For example, they recognize the service of history as the remembrancer and recorder of what Sidney terms
"the particular truth of things." [151] Witness the fact that in
time's record-book or "tables," according to Shakespeare,
are written not only such "tell-tale" memories as may

> repeat and history [old] loss
> To new remembrance,[152]

but also "true rules" and "statutes": "the voice of the recorded law" which rebellious scoundrels such as Jack Cade
would, if they could, silence forever when seeking to subvert
the state and to subject England's ancient liberties to the
crazy rule of mob dictatorship: "Burn all the records of the
realm! My mouth shall be the parliament of England." [153]
Sidney, further, admits that "old-aged experience" "of true

matters" — that is to say, the actuality of history — has its points, at least for "gross" conceits. In other words, the observation of history that such and such a thing actually *"was done* doth warrant a man more" as to what *"shall follow"* in times to come, even if he should naïvely "argue, because it rained yesterday, therefore it should rain today." [154] Shakespeare sets forth this principle more positively and generously:

> There is a history in all men's lives . . .
> The which observ'd, a man may prophesy,
> With a near aim, of the main chance of things
> As yet not come to life.[155]

On the whole, however, our poets do not go out of their way to praise history. Shakespeare, of course, does not specifically argue the case against it, any more than he argues the case against philosophy. But his historical plays in particular, and a good many of his other plays here and there, touch upon many of Sidney's favorite exceptions against history and the historians: their reliance upon "hearsay" masquerading as "authority," their tedious literalness, and their lack of impartiality, imaginative insight, and power.

Sidney airs most of these objections immediately after he has paid his respects to the sullen gravity of the moral philosophers. "The historian," we read,[156] "scarcely giveth leisure" to the philosophers to state their case before asserting "in a great chafe" that "for teaching of virtue, and virtuous actions" none "is comparable to him." This in spite of the fact that the historian is poorly equipped to substantiate his claims. For he comes to court "loaden with old *mouse-eaten records,* authorizing himself (for the most part) upon other histories, whose greatest *authorities* are built upon the notable foundation of *hearsay*, having much ado to accord differing writers and to pick truth out of *partiality*, better acquainted with a thousand years ago than with the present age, and yet better knowing how this world goeth" — which, as King Lear says, "a man may see . . . with no eyes" [157] — "than how his own wit runneth." In short, the historians are (1) untrustworthy: biased in attitude or unreliable in their treatment of sources; (2) blindly or stupidly imcompetent: incapable of interpreting for the present age the meaning of times past. Directly or indirectly both counts of this indictment appear also in Shakespeare.

The plays and sonnets frequently remind one of the *Defense* because they, too, reveal something of the creative artist's instinctive distaste for the musty or dry-as-dust materials [158] of conventional history. I refer especially to Sidney's "mouse-eaten records" — "picked," in Shakespeare's equally incisive phrase,

> from the wormholes of long-vanish'd days,
> . . . from the dust of old oblivion rak'd.[159]

Again, I recall the outspoken utterances of Berowne and Lafew against pedantic learning in general, and their particular dislike of that painful culling of "authorities" by "all the learned and authentic fellows" [160] who "seek the light of truth" meekly, by accepting the say-so of "others' books," or, like Sidney's friends, have "much ado to accord differing writers":

> Small have continual plodders ever won
> Save base authority from others' books.[161]

It is *base* authority in another sense because, as Sidney says, it too often relies on hearsay, and is often inspired by casual

rumor or calculated falsehood. It is made of the very stuff
which Shakespeare dramatized unforgettably in the Prologue
to the second part of *King Henry IV* and in the events which
make good this Prologue's prophecy — the prophecy of
"Rumour, painted full of tongues":

> Open your ears, for which of you will stop
> The vent of hearing when loud Rumour speaks?
> I from the Orient to the drooping West,
> Making the wind my posthorse, still unfold
> The acts commenced on this ball of earth.
> Upon my tongues continual slanders ride,
> The which in every language I pronounce,
> Stuffing the ears of men with false reports.

The currency of false report, however, is not to be
charged merely to the foolish actions of the wavering multi-
tude. According to Sidney the "partiality" and the stupid
ineptitude of the chroniclers are to blame, and here again
Shakespeare agrees. Once or twice, to be sure, he pays his
respects to "good" or "honest" chroniclers.[162] But he speaks
more often of those who trim up the praises of their favorites
with false adulation, making their

> chronicle as rich with praise
> As is the ooze and bottom of the sea
> With sunken wrack and sumless treasuries.[163]

Again, he alludes to other chroniclers who mercilessly "tra-
duce" their victims, as Wolsey protests that he is,

> Traduc'd by ignorant tongues, which neither know
> My faculties nor person yet will be
> The chronicles of my doing.[164]

Of course Sidney is right in observing that such writers as
these are ill prepared to perform the tasks of the true his-

torian. "Although . . . verity be written in their foreheads"
they do not know how "to pick truth out of" [165] the controversial raw material, the debatable records of history. Let us
note, once more, that a cogent observation to much the same
effect appears in Shakespeare. The "wise" young Prince of
Wales in *Richard III* [166] raises the question whether Julius
Caesar built the Tower of London. On being told that Caesar began it, he wants to know whether this information is
derived from recorded data or from popular tradition. He is
advised that the information is "upon record." Then, still
skeptical, he insists that historical truth should come out at
long last, whether or not it be actually "registered" in the
books:

> *Prince*: Is it upon record, or else reported
> Successively from age to age, he built it?
> *Buckingham*: Upon record, my gracious lord.
> *Prince*: But say, my lord, it were not regist'red,
> Methinks the truth should live from age to age
> As 'twere retail'd to all posterity,
> Even to the general all-ending day.

In the final analysis history must, indeed, bear more than
its adventitious burden of dubious records and poorly quali-
fied interpreters; it must also reckon with its indigenous limitations. Shakespeare, I think, hints at some of them when
he suggests that sometimes, in the depths of the human spirit,
there is an unspoken history which no ordinary historian can
write and which challenges even the resources of the poet.
Such is the history, for example, of Cordelia's deep affec-
tions; her reticence of spirit,

> a tardiness in nature
> Which often leaves the history unspoke
> That it intends to do. [167]

And such is the story of Hermione's suffering,

> which is more
> Than history can pattern, though devis'd
> And play'd to take spectators.[168]

The essential implications of these passages Sidney [169] had anticipated again and again. History cannot do what only great poetry can do. History is tied to the "bare *Was*" of literal reality, "captived to the truth of a foolish world." Poetry, Aristotle had said, is "more philosophical" than history. It is so, according to Sidney, because only "the peerless poet" *by virtue of his creative imagination*,[170] can transcend reality, unite the philosopher's precepts with the historian's examples, and better them both by his own "feigned" examples, characters, and stories. "The best of the historian," in particular, "is subject to the poet," because the latter can "make his own" whatsoever fact or act the historian has to offer, "beautifying it both for future teaching, and more delighting." The historian must record not — what "should be," but what "was": too often "events whereof he can yield no cause" and fortune's frequent favors to the wicked. But the poet can render poetic justice, "see virtue exalted and vice punished," and enchant young and old with his divine vision, his music, and his irresistible tales.

Shakespeare, as I have said, does not argue this case, but he makes it his own. Though Cleopatra, for example, observes that "some innocents scape not the thunderbolt,"[171] no one who reads Shakespeare fairly can doubt that poetic justice essentially controls his disposition of men and events, not only in the great tragedies but also in the historical plays — in *Richard II*, *Richard III*, and the *Henry IV* group hardly less than in *Othello* and *Macbeth*. For the rest, we have seen that the chorus-prologues in *Henry V* emphasize, almost as vigorously as Sidney himself, the essential contribution of the creative imagination — in poet and audience — to the poet's high purpose of making history live and "move." (Even those who "have . . . read the story" must see it, live it "in the quick forge and working house of thought.") [172] Again, it goes almost without saying that Shakespeare, in his treatment of historical events and persons, was not "captived" to the "bare *Was*" of literal fact. Some of his "feigned" episodes — for example, the plucking of the red rose and the white in *1 Henry VI*,[173] the gardeners' scene in *Richard II* [174] — have more essential truth in them than most of the historians' "verities." He makes Prince Arthur and Hotspur younger, and King Henry IV and Richard II's queen older than they were in the chronicles, and thereby dramatically and humanly more significant. Whatsoever he found in the chronicles and in his other sources he made "his own." Thus, for example, he transformed Oldcastle-Fastolfe into Falstaff. And thus, because he was a peerless poet and indeed "the monarch" of all the history and all the humanity he surveyed, his people — Falstaff and Cleopatra and the rest — so live that, in Sidney's words,[175] "we seem not to hear *of* them, but clearly to *see through them*." And "their names" have become household words.

DEFENSE: PART TWO

Something remains to be said concerning the second part of the *Defense*, the shortest and the least excursive of the three parts of that essay. Here Sidney [1] refutes the strictures of Gosson-and-company against poetry. Their "low-creeping objections," he wrote, are "soon trodden down." He was able to make short work of them, partly because he had already put them under heavy fire in the first part of the *Defense*. However, even if we had not just reviewed that part, we could hardly expect Part Two to be equal in importance, for our purposes, with Parts One and Three. They are concerned with poetic form and technique, not almost exclusively — as is the present part — with controversial critical attitudes. This part has less relation to Shakespeare than the others, for Shakespeare was essentially a dramatist and storyteller who rarely made much of contemporary controversy for its own sake. Temperamentally and professionally he was not another Ben Jonson. We get from him, at most, only an occasional allusion to the contemporary wars of the theatre; [2] and we can hardly expect more than occasional sideglances at the contemporary wars of the critics. Yet these sideglances may not be negligible in sum total, nor without significant relationship to the *Defense*. I shall take them into account in summarizing Sidney's answers to the "poet-haters."

Answer number one,[3] for example, need not detain us long. For Sidney had previously taken sufficient account of the "pleasant fault-finders' " favorite "scorning humours" concerning "rhyming and versing." In other words, he had "already said" — and Shakespeare, as I have suggested, had substantially agreed — that "it is not rhyming and versing that maketh poesy," [4] though true rhyme and verse are among its greatest gifts.

Next come the "most important imputations" — four in number — "against the poor poets": (1) that "many other . . . knowledges" are "more fruitful" than poetry; (2) that poetry is "the mother of lies"; (3) that poetry "is the nurse of" other sinful "abuse"; (4) that "Plato banished" the poets "out of his commonwealth." [5]

I shall glance at these four items in the sequence indicated, except that I shall begin by dismissing item 4, concerning Plato. I do so for two reasons. First: Shakespeare does not name Plato. It may not be amiss, however, to recall that he also fails to name Chaucer and Spenser, though he almost certainly knew these poets.[6] Moreover, Berowne and his fellows in their "little Academe" of *Love's Labour's Lost* [7] had doubtless heard of Plato in their time. Even so, since Shakespeare does not argue against Plato's proscription of the poets, I shall not rehearse the details of Sidney's answer. Second: Suffice it to say that the gist of that answer[8] (Plato, himself the "most poetical" of philosophers, in certain places actually gives "high . . . commendation to poetry," and, at worst, banished not poetry but "the abuse" thereof) is close to Sidney's and Shakespeare's general statement of the case for poetry as against philosophy. That case has been discussed above.[9] Here I would add only that "Plato, being a philosopher, was" according to Sidney,[10] "a natural enemy of poets," and that Shakespeare reminiscently dramatized the antipathy between poet and philosopher in *Timon*.[11] Our poets honored learning and "philosophical instructions"; but, being neither "stoics nor . . . stocks" themselves, they made short work of the philosophers' narrow and unphilosophical "objections" to poetry.

I turn, next, to the three remaining imputations against the poets: (1) The charge that other knowledge is more fruitful than poetry. Here again my own notes on Sidney's earlier pages, and on Shakespeare's probable reactions thereto, will suffice for our purposes. Since no other learning can "teach and *move* . . . to [virtue] so much as poetry," clearly "there is" not "sprung out of earth a more fruitful knowlege" than poetry.[12]

(2) To the next charge — that the poets are the "principal liars" — Sidney replies that "of all writers under the sun the poet is the least liar."[13] This is so because astronomers, geometricians, physicians, historians, and all the rest, make definite, but sometimes questionable, affirmations, whereas "the poet . . . never affirmeth . . . . never maketh any circles about your imagination to conjure you to believe for" literal truth the "invention[s]" "the sweet muses . . . inspire in . . . him." By way of proof two illustrations (to which I have already referred) are offered. The first makes the point that even a child "coming to a play" doesn't believe it is in Thebes just because it sees "Thebes" written in great letters on the stage — any more than Shakespeare's audience, crammed into the Globe's "wooden O," believed that the stage actually encompassed the vasty field of Agincourt.[14] The second illustration admits, with Shakespeare,

that the poet's imagination does give a local habitation and a name to its fictions, but denies that any "falsehood" is involved in this gift. "The poets give names" ("Cyrus or Aeneas"), in order to give their brain children a recognizable place in the world of men: "To make their picture the more lively . . . not to build any history." [15] Let us also recall that Shakespeare repeatedly returned to this charge of falsehood against the poets. In *Timon* the lie is passed in both directions. The poet, as noted above,[16] brands the philosopher a liar because the latter charged the poet with falsehood for addressing him as "philosopher." The Philosopher's retort sums up the ancient libel against the poets in a word:

> *Apemantus*: Art not a poet?
> *Poet*:   Yes.
> *Apemantus*: Then thou liest.[17]

Touchstone's remarks to the ingenuous Audrey convey the same general meaning — albeit with a difference, since Touchstone himself is not the worst of poets. "Now, if thou wert a poet, I might have some hope thou didst feign." This, says Professor Kittredge,[18] is "the orthodox Platonic doctrine that all poets are liars." But of course Touchstone is here talking with his tongue in his cheek. He had spoken seriously a moment earlier, when he told the same Audrey, in effect, what Sidney had so eloquently urged,[19] that true poetry is essentially imaginative: "Truest poetry is the most feigning." [20]

(3) The final count in the indictment [21] is that poetry "abuseth man's wit, training it to wanton sinfulness and lustful love." Of this general charge Sidney is willing to "grant" only so much as to deprecate, with Shakespeare,[22]

certain excesses in one or another of the "kinds or species" of poetry, for example, in "the lyric . . . larded with passionate" (or "wailful") [23] "sonnets," and in "the elegiac" when it "weeps" too copiously or too "woefully." By and large, however, Sidney stoutly denies the allegation. At worst, he says, the truth is "not . . . that poetry abuseth man's wit, but that man's wit abuseth poetry." Specifically, he discusses three aspects of this abuse of poetry, as follows.

First: He admits [24] that "man's wit may make poesy . . . *fantastic*," [25] and that poetry, so abused, "by . . . reason of his sweet charming force can do more hurt than any other *army of words*." I have already noted that Shakespeare also used the phrase here italicized,[26] and I need scarcely add that this was not the only occasion on which he, too, spoke out against fantastical wordiness or "vain fantasy" in general, and particularly against the "high-fantastical" aberrations of unrestrained poetic "fancy." [27]

Second: Sidney [28] repeatedly and sharply denies that "the abuse of a thing" can reasonably "make the right use odious." Indeed, he argues, that which "abused, doth most harm . . . rightly used . . . doth most good." Except as just indicated, in connection with the aberrations of poetic fancy, Shakespeare does not enlarge upon the specific antithesis between poetry abused and poetry rightly used. It may be worth noting, however, that the general antithesis between "right use" [29] and "abuse" appears over and over again in his pages.[30] So, too, does Sidney's observation that the highest faculties or institutions, human and divine, are most liable to abuse. "Doth not . . . law . . . abused," Sidney had asked, "grow the crooked fosterer of horrible injuries? Doth not . . . God's word abused breed heresy?" Bassanio, before choosing the leaden casket, asks virtually the same question:

> In law, what plea so tainted and corrupt
> But, being season'd with a gracious voice,
> Obscures the show of evil? In religion,
> What damned error but some sober brow
> Will bless it and approve it with a text? [31]

Third: Sidney [32] steadfastly urges that the true use of imagination is essential to poetry, though the abuse of imagination — by fantastic wit — is an abuse to poetry. But he denies utterly that good poetry in and by itself abuses men by over-indulging their imagination and causing them (in Hamlet's words) [33] to "lose the name of action." The poet-haters "allege" that poetry "hath set their heart's delight" not "upon action" — as of old, "before poets began to be in price" — but "upon imagination." But "no memory is so ancient" as to be able to recall a "before time" when poets were *not* "in price." In short, this objection, first and last, is merely "the ordinary doctrine of ignorance," "a chain-shot against all learning" — this learning which even Juliet's nurse applauded with all her heart.[34] Poetry, this *best* learning, won Alexander the Great to prefer "dead Homer" to "living Aristotle." In a word, poetry — as Sidney's own life and death well proved — does *not* unfit men for action: time made good his observation, in the *Defense*, that "poetry is," properly speaking, "the *companion* of the camps." [35] Let us note, finally, that Hotspur's pre-battle invective against Glendower does not seriously undermine this principle. In fact Hotspur does not deny that the Welsh poet-warrior is "valiant as a lion" in spite of his dreams and verses.[36] Perhaps Hotspur objects primarily to "mincing" poetry, rather than to poetry in general. In any other sense his own words — like Plato's and Hamlet's [37] — belie him, for he was a true poet [38] in his own right.

CONCLUDING NOTE

It was Dr. Johnson the philosopher rather than Dr. Johnson the scholar who boldly entitled his last chapter of *Rasselas*, "The Conclusion, in which Nothing is Concluded." Perhaps it is foolhardy to recall this fact, but any healthy skeptic who has followed me thus far is welcome to such aid and comfort as he may derive from Dr. Johnson's caption. For the conclusions of this study, however, he will need to turn to the preceding chapters. I hope the evidence therein presented has spoken for itself. What little I have to add is written chiefly to reëmphasize main objectives, implications, or points of direction as I see them.

My basic purpose throughout has been to "join the precepts" of the greatest critic of the English Renaissance with the "examples" of its mightiest poet: to illustrate the significant but hitherto undemonstrated truth that Shakespeare — for whatever reason, casually or causally — "executed" what Sidney had "outlined." So far the study should prove valid for all concerned, the more so because it endeavors to recognize fairly not only the likenesses but also the differences between the poets (for example, their treatment of imagination in poetry). Incidentally, this essay has sought to give valid emphasis to another fact which still needs to be underscored: the fact that Shakespeare had vastly more critical sensitivity and outspokenness than has generally been recognized. It is not for me to cast stones, but I will add that because of Sidney's consistently discursive and often redundant method, the task of arranging my findings has not proved easy. I have tried to hew to the line, and I trust that I have not added too many sins of my own to those of Sir Philip. I hope in any case, that the reader will have found in my analyses of Sidney's and Shakespeare's comments a compensating comprehensiveness of matter and freshness of emphasis.

In my judgment, finally, the evidence adduced in this study indicates not only that Shakespeare illustrated Sidney, but that he remembered him. Of course a literary relationship — and more especially a literary indebtedness — cannot, as a rule, be demonstrated as neatly as a proposition in Euclid. I have called attention to many likenesses which I believe to be significant — likenesses ("parallels") between our poets in word, phrase or cadence, imagery and thought, mood and attitude. Yet I would be the last to deny that real difficulties are involved in any argument from "parallels"; indeed I am informed that the parallel proposition is debatable even in Euclid. Full allowance must certainly be made: (1) for errors in judgment on the part of students who may tend to find likenesses chiefly because they are looking for them; (2) for that perverse trick of human nature in scholarship whereby "everybody uses parallel passages, but mistrusts them in the hands of another"; [39] (3) for common sources [40] and chance likenesses. With regard to the latter, I do not forget Tennyson's comment upon certain "bookworms" who "will not allow one to say 'Ring the bells' without finding that we have taken it from Sir P. Sidney," [41] nor do I forget similar protests from English masters in prose and verse from Sir Thomas Browne [42] to Byron [43] and William Morris.[44] But these objections ignore two facts which also deserve due weight. First, as Milton suggested,[45] what "good authors" borrow may be "bettered" in the "borrowing." Second — in spite of Tennyson's understandable annoyance — Shelley,[46] and, in our time, T. S. Eliot,[47] remind us that poets in general are "a very camœleonic race" and do tend to take "the colour of what they feed on." We know that the Elizabethans "habitually quoted each other — without giving credit — to an extent that is unbelievable today." [48] Shakespeare in particular is no exception to the rule. Of course his quasi-acknowledgment in Sonnet 76 — "All my best is dressing old words new" — is not to be taken literally,[49] but his habit of picking up phrases, not only from the chroniclers but from his greater and lesser contemporaries, Marlowe, Spenser, Daniel, and the rest, is as familiar as it is felicitous. The reader will hardly escape the conviction that the likenesses between Sidney and Shakespeare are too pervasive and far-reaching to be accidental. He will have seen that they are not hazy or unsupported "parallels" projected into or from the circumambient unknown. All the antecedent probabilities indicate that, if Shakespeare read anything, he could not have been ignorant of the *Defense*. His fellow poets and dramatists knew the treatise and used it. He himself knew and used the *Arcadia*. Mr. Maxwell Anderson, to take a modern instance, knows his *Hamlet*. To suppose that Shakespeare, knowing the *Arcadia*, was ignorant of the *Defense*, is like supposing that the author of *Winterset* had never heard of *Romeo and Juliet*.

NOTES

Consistent with the normal practice of modernizing spelling in quotations from Shakespeare, the text and notes modernize spelling in quotations from Sidney. Also, in order to emphasize a point, the writer has frequently italicized words not italicized in the original.

CHAPTER I

[1] *The Schoolmaster* (1570); G. Gregory Smith, *Elizabethan Critical Essays* (1904), I, 12. (This volume, which includes the text of the *Defense* here used, is hereafter cited as "Smith.")

[2] For significant modern instances, cf. G. C. Taylor's analysis in *Philological Quarterly*, XXII (1943), 330 ff.

[3] Smith, I, 8.

[4] Smith, I, 21.

[5] Boston (1890), p. v.

[6] Cf. H. R. D. Anders, *Shakespeare's Books* (1904), pp. 102–103; E. K. Chambers, *Shakespeare* (1930), I, 407, 470, 490, 527.

[7] Occasional glosses in Cook's edition, quoted or credited below, are exceptions to the rule, but virtually none touch upon the specific question of influence with reference to the *Defense*. So far as I can discover, not a word on the subject appears, for example, in the works mentioned in n. 6 above, nor in David Klein's *Literary Criticism in the Elizabethan Dramatists* (1910), W. H. Bond's recent dissertation, "The Reputation and Influence of Sir Philip Sidney" (unpublished, Harvard, 1941), in the Furness Variorum and other standard editions of Shakespeare, nor in the standard editions of the *Defense* such as Smith's, Flügel's, Shuckburgh's, J. C. Collins', and Feuillerat's. For a review of the discussion of Shakespeare as an "unconscious" or "conscious" artist, see Thaler, "Shakespeare on Style, Imagination, and Poetry," *Shakespeare and Democracy* (1941), especially pp. 62–74.

[8] Sidney "is not so much a critic as an interpreter and prophet," J. C. Collins, Sidney's *Apology* (Oxford, 1907), p. xxvii.

[9] Smith, I, 390; Cook, p. 90.

[10] For the passage in Harington see Smith, II, 208.

[11] Smith, I, 171–172.

[12] In this case I find one exception on each side: Dover Wilson and Quiller-Couch, in their (Cambridge University Press, 1923) ed. of *Love's Labour's Lost*, p. 141, and on the other side, William Gray in his ed. of the *Miscellaneous Works of Sir Philip Sidney* (Boston, 1860), p. 85 n.

[13] Smith, I, 173–174.

[14] Smith, I, 175; in other words, the pastoral's "*pretty tales* of wolves and sheep" figuring forth the "whole considerations of wrong doing and patience." Cf. Smith, I, 167: "*Pretty* allegories . . . for-mal *tales.*" Editors have no comment on this recurring phrase, nor upon its Shakespearean counterpart. See also n. 17 below.

[15] I have joined, at the end of the quotation, lines 153 and 115.

[16] It appears in Livy, Dionysius of Halicarnassus, North's Plutarch (1579): "All the members of man's body did rebel against the belly, complaining . . . that it only remained in the midst of the body with-out doing anything"; Camden's *Remains* (1605): "All the members of the body conspired against the stomach as against the swallowing gulf of all their labours." Douce and Chambers regard these two passages as Shakespeare's source. For summaries of documents and discussion see Furness Variorum, *Coriolanus*, p. 33, and, especially, E. K. Chambers in the American Arden edition of *Coriolanus*, pp. 194 ff., 160.

[17] Cf. previous note. Furness found the phrase, "A pretty tale," twice repeated in North's translation of *The Fables of Bidpai* (1570). This "indicate[s]," he writes, a Shakespearean "recollection of this translation by North," even though "the rest of the fable" in this translation "is in no way like to that in the other collections." Fur-ness overlooked the fact that this phrase is also twice repeated in the *Defense* (see above, n. 14), and that Sidney's adjective "mutinous" is twice repeated by Shakespeare (see quotation on p. 6).

[18] Smith, I, 391; Cook, p. 92; Collins, p. 83.

[19] See above, n. 16.

[20] *2 Henry IV*, III, ii, 76–78. (Cf. Sidney's remark on the "stately speeches and well sounding phrases" of *Gorboduc*, Smith, I, 196.)

[21] Cf. Cook, pp. xx–xxi; Smith, I, xc, etc.

[22] *Complete Works of Shakespeare*, ed. G. L. Kittredge (1936), p. 624.

[23] "The earliest recorded instance of this figurative use" (Cook, p. 103. No mention of *The Merchant of Venice*). I append, for what they may be worth, three additional likenesses in figure or phrase:

(1) *Defense* (Smith, I, 160):
The final end [of learning] is to
lead and draw us to as high a
perfection as our *degenerate
souls,* made *worse* by their
clayey lodgings, can be capable
of.

Merchant, V, i, 63–65:
Such harmony is in immortal
souls;
But whilst this *muddy vesture
of decay*
Doth *grossly* close it in, we
cannot hear it.

(2) *Defense* (Smith, I, 186):
That *lovely* name of *love* . . .

3 Henry VI, V, vii, 26:
. . . *love* my *lovely* queen.

(3) *Defense* (Smith, I, 193):
Anciently . . . *great captains*
[not only favoured poets, but
were poets].

Othello, II, i, 74:
Our *great captain's* captain.

---

[24] Cf. Thaler, *Shakespeare and Democracy,* p. 83; and *Publications
of the Modern Language Association,* LIII (1938), 1019 ff.

[25] See above, pp. 18 ff., 42 ff., etc.

[26] Sidney reiterates the last phrase here italicized. (See above p. 9,
item (a) 2, and Smith, I, 158, 164: "A speaking picture . . . to teach
and delight"; "A perfect picture, I say.")

[27] Cook, p. xxxix.

[28] See below, Chap. II, n. 44; Chap. III, nn. 24, 48.

[29] Shelley, at the time of writing his *Defense of Poetry,* "was familiar with . . . and had been only recently re-reading" Sidney's essay
(N. I. White, *Shelley,* New York, 1940, II, 271–272, 609).

[30] Quoted by N. I. White, II, 609, from the *Works of Shelley,* Ju-
lian ed. (London, 1926–1930), X, 283.

[31] Smith, I, xci–xcii.

[32] Sidney's *Miscellaneous Works,* ed. Gray, p. 337.

[33] See above, n. 10; Cook, p. xxxix; E. S. Shuckburgh, Sidney's
Apologie (Pitt Press Series, London, 1891), p. 155.

[34] For Churchyard, Vaughan, and Wither, see Bond, I, 96 ff. On
Drayton and Spenser, see Cook, pp. 128, 126. Cook, however, does
not note the likeness between the following passage from the *Defense*
and Spenser's remark in his letter to Raleigh dated January 23, 1589:

Defense (Smith, I, 168–169):
History . . . say[s] . . . *such a
thing was done* . . . . but . . . .

A Letter of the Author's [of *The
Faerie Queen*] to Sir Walter Raleigh (Greenlaw, Osgood, Pad-

the best of the historian is subject to the poet; for whatsoever action . . . the historian is bound to recite, that may the poet . . . make his own; beautifying it both for further teaching and more delighting, as *it pleaseth him.*

elford, Variorum *Spenser*, 1932, I, 168–169):

An historiographer discourseth of affairs orderly *as they were done* . . . but a poet thrusteth into the midst . . . recoursing to the things forepast, and divining of things to come, *maketh a pleasing analysis* of all.

On Nashe, see *Library of Old English Prose Writers* (Cambridge, England, 1831), II, xliii; on Jonson, see text, and notes below.

[35] According to Fuller's account. (Cf. J. Q. Adams, *Life of Shakespeare*, 1923, p. 242.)

[36] Smith, I, 196 ff.; see above, pp. 18 ff. While seeing these notes through the press, I find my judgment as to the general probability of Shakespeare's knowing the *Defense* independently confirmed in E. M. W. Tillyard's *Shakespeare's History Plays* (New York, 1946), p. 4: "Shakespeare . . . . might have read of it [the doctrine of the dramatic unities] in Sidney; he might have heard it discussed . . . . it is . . . improbable that he could have avoided acquaintance with it in [these] two ways."

[37] J. E. Spingarn, *Literary Criticism of the Renaissance* (1930), p. 278. Cf. *Timber*, ed. F. E. Schelling (Boston, 1892), pp. 73 ff.

[38] Frank Mathew, *An Image of Shakespeare* (London, 1922), pp. 227–228. See Jonson, *The Poetaster*, in Herford and Simpson, *Jonson* (1925), IV, 204. For the following quotation from Sidney, see Smith, I, 205.

[39] For the passages just quoted from the *Defense*, see Smith, I, 197, 199.

[40] See Herford and Simpson, *Jonson*, III, 303. Smith (I, 399; II, 389) quotes and discusses the passage in illustration of the *Defense*. With reference to the last line quoted from Jonson, cf. Sidney: "Comedy is an imitation of the common errors of our life"; "the great fault [in comedies is] that they stir laughter in sinful things . . . rather execrable than ridiculous." (Smith, I, 176, 200.)

[41] Smith, I, 182.

[42] See Herford and Simpson, *Jonson*, V, 186. For this reference I am indebted to Bond, I, 102.

[43] Spingarn, p. 268.

[44] For other reasons see the discussion mentioned in n. 7, above.

CHAPTER II

[1] These are italicized in Cook's edition, pp. 31, 44, 57. Cf. Smith, I, 180, 193, 205. Professor K. O. Myrick finds in the *Defense* "unmistakable" signs of "all the" *seven or eight* formal "parts of a carefully elaborated classical oration" (*Sir Philip Sidney as a Literary Craftsman*, 1935, pp. 53–82). But Sidney's three summaries unmistakably mark the three major divisions of his essay.

[2] Indebted, in part, to Shuckburgh's (p. xxxiv) and Cook's (pp. xli–xlv).

[3] Smith, I, 175.

[4] Smith, I, 196, 201.

[5] The subject immediately preceding Sidney's remarks on tragedy and comedy should be mentioned here. In a short paragraph (Smith, I, 196) he pays tribute, with some reservations, to Chaucer (*Troilus*), Spenser (*The Shepherd's Calendar*), *The Mirror for Magistrates*, and to Surrey's lyrics, as the chief earlier fruits of English poetry. Shakespeare also knew and alluded to all of these — and also to Gower, who is mentioned earlier in the *Defense* (Smith, I, 152) — though he does not discuss their merits and defects. (On Shakespeare and Chaucer, cf., *Complete Shakespeare*, Kittredge ed., p. 229, and Hyder E. Rollins, *PMLA*, XXXII (1917), 383 ff.; on Shakespeare and Spenser, cf. Thaler, *Shakespeare Association Bulletin*, X (1935), 192–211, XI (1936), 33–40, *Shakespeare and Democracy*, pp. 106–118; on Shakespeare and the *Mirror*, cf. F. E. Schelling, *The English Chronicle Play* (1902), pp. 36, 192, and Willard Farnham, *Medieval Heritage of Elizabethan Tragedy* (1936), pp. 271 ff.; on Shakespeare and Surrey, see below n. 77; on Gower, see *Pericles*.)

[6] Smith, I, 177; cf. above, p. 7, item b.

[7] "The poets . . . have . . . put never more pious words in the mouth of any person than of a tyrant. I shall not instance an abstruse author . . . but . . . William Shakespeare, who introduces . . . Richard the Third speaking in . . . a [high] strain of piety and mortification . . .

> I do not know that Englishman alive
> With whom my soul is any jot at odds . . .
> I thank my God for my humility.
> [*Richard III*, II, i, 69–72.]

Other stuff of this sort may be read throughout the whole tragedy"
(Milton's *Prose Works*, ed. J. A. St. John, 1893, I, 326–327).

[8] Smith, I, 177.

[9] *Richard III*, I, iii, 259, iv, 78; 2 *Henry IV*, III, i, 31.

[10] Smith, I, 170. (Cf. Clarence's dream of his agony "after life,"
Richard III, I, iv, 43–57.) On this theme see also Sir Thomas Elyot,
The Governor, ed. H.H.S. Croft (1880), I, 71 (cited by Shuck-
burgh, p. 114).

[11] Smith, I, 190, 178.

[12] Cf. Professor Kittredge's note on *Hamlet*, II, ii, 617–620, in his
ed. (1939), pp. 204–205.

[13] *Love's L. L.*, IV, iii, 348–349.

[14] *Henry V*, Chorus, II, line 6.

[15] Translated by Cyril Connolly (New York, 1944), p. 27.

[16] *Macbeth*, IV, iii, 178–179; V, ii, 16–18; V, iii, 23.

[17] To which Shakespeare alludes in *Twelfth Night*, IV, ii, 16: "a
niece of King Gorboduc."

[18] *Sir Philip Sidney's Astrophel and Stella und The Defense of
Poesie*, ed. E. Flügel (Halle, 1889), p. xlvi.

[19] Smith, I, 155; the preceding quotations from the *Defense* in this
paragraph: Smith, I, 161, 165–166, 196–197.

[20] " 'Imitatio vitae . . . imago veritatis.' This phrase ascribed by
Donatus to Cicero, runs through all the dramatic discussions of the
Renaissance, and finds its echo in a famous passage in *Hamlet*"
(Spingarn, p. 104). Before Sidney, Sir Thomas Elyot had written:
"Comedies . . . be . . . a mirror of man's life" (*The Governor*, ed.
Croft, I, 124; cited by Shuckburgh, p. 111).

[21] Cf. the *Defense*: to "see virtue exalted and vice punished . . . that
commendation is peculiar to poetry" (Smith, I, 170).

[22] *Hamlet*, III, ii, 23–28. "It is significant that Shakespeare follows
closely" Sidney's "observations as to the 'purpose of playing' " to the
effect that "we should see 'all the virtues, vices and passions laid to
the view' " (R. Eagle, *Baconiana*, XIII, 1915, 154 ff.).

[23] Sidney: "A tragedy is tied to the laws of poesy" (Smith, I, 198);
Jonson (Prologue to *Volpone*): "The laws of time, place, persons,
he observeth"; Shakespeare (in the speech of Polonius quoted in the
next paragraph): "the law of writ."

[24] Smith, I, 159.

[25] Smith, I, 175.

[26] On Plautus and Seneca in the *Defense*, see Smith, I, 198, 197.

[27] *Hamlet*, II, ii, 415–420.

[28] See above, pp. 22 ff.

[29] Smith, I, 199.

[30] Spingarn, p. 282.

[31] *Hamlet* (1939), p. 195.

[32] See above, p. 11, and Chap. I, nn. 36, 39.

[33] Yet Shakespeare, like most good dramatists, frequently uses a venerable device for drawing time and place together. As Sidney says, "Many things may be told which cannot be showed. . . . so was the manner the ancients took, by some Nuncius to recount things done in former time or other place" (Smith, I, 198). For Shakespeare's use of the messenger device, cf. *1 Henry VI*, I, i; *2 Henry IV*, I, i; *Macbeth*, IV, iii; *Antony and Cleopatra*, II, v; etc.

[34] *Complete Shakespeare*, p. 624. Quoted by permission of the publisher, Ginn and Company.

[35] *Henry V*, Prologue, 11–13; Choruses, II, 32, V, 3–6:

> I humbly pray [those who know their history] to admit
>   th' excuse
> Of time, of numbers, and due course of things
> Which cannot in their huge and proper life
> Be here presented.

(Cf. Shuckburgh, p. 151, and Thaler, *Shakespeare and Democracy*, p. 81.) Sidney himself partly "admitted" the force of this "excuse" (see Smith, I, 185, quoted above, p. 44).

[36] *Henry V*, Prologue, line 25; Choruses, IV, 49–53, III, 7; Prologue, line 23; Chorus II, 6.

[37] *Preface to Shakespeare* (1765).

[38] *Henry V*, Prologue, lines 30–31. The three lines quoted just below are from Chorus, III, 1–3.

[39] *Romeo and Juliet*, Prologue, line 12. Cf. Sidney's "two hours' space" (Smith, I, 197, quoted above, p. 11).

[40] See also *Pericles*, Prologues III, 12–14, IV, 47–50; IV, iv, 1–7. (Cf. Klein, p. 69.)

[41] Cf. *Timon of Athens*, I, i, 37:

> Artificial strife
> Lives in these touches, livelier than life.

[42] Smith, I, 195.

[43] Smith, I, 195–196. See also pp. 201, 204: "Words but never matter"; "The right use of both matter and manner."

⁴⁴ Horace, unlike Sidney and Shakespeare, virtually suggests that if the poet chooses proper matter, the words will all but take care of themselves:

> *rem tibi Socraticae poterunt ostendere chartae,*
> *verbaque provisam rem non invita sequentur*

(*Ars Poetica*, lines 310–311; *The Art of Poetry*, ed. A. S. Cook, New York, 1926, p. 23).

⁴⁵ *Hamlet*, II, ii, 194; V, ii, 166; II, ii, 95; II, ii, 463; *King Lear*, I, i, 56. See also *Merchant*, III, v, 73–75: "Fools . . . that for a tricksy word/Defy the matter."

⁴⁶ Smith, I, 199.

⁴⁷ *Hamlet*, III, ii, 19–50; II, ii, 462.

⁴⁸ Smith, I, 199.

⁴⁹ Mathew, p. 288. See above, pp. 78, n. 38; 7 (a).

⁵⁰ Whetstone, Dedication to *Promos and Cassandra* (1578), in Smith, I, 60 (cf. Klein, pp. 25, 30); Gascoigne, *Certain Notes of Instruction* (1575). For the passage quoted immediately below, see Smith, I, 48.

⁵¹ Smith, I, 199–201.

⁵² Though there are one or two bits of grim humor in the remarks of the murderers of Clarence (*Richard III*, I, iv, 102–131), these murderers are not clowns.

⁵³ Cf. the title page in J. Q. Adams, *Chief Pre-Shakespearean Dramas* (1924), p. 638.

⁵⁴ *1 Henry IV*, II, iv, 425–426.

⁵⁵ Smith, I, 196, and, for the passages next summarized, I, 176–177.

⁵⁶ *Taming of the Shrew*, Induction, ii, 139–144.

⁵⁷ As: "A Christmas comedy" of "some slight zany . . . some trencher knight" (*Love's L. L.*, V, ii, 462–464).

⁵⁸ Cf. J. Dover Wilson, *The Essential Shakespeare* (1932), p. 10.

⁵⁹ "Pat he comes, like the catastrophe in the old comedy" (*Lear*, I, ii, 146).

⁶⁰ *Taming*, Induction, ii, 132.

⁶¹ *A Midsummer Night's Dream*, IV, ii, 45.

⁶² *3 Henry VI*, V, vii, 43–44 (cf. Klein, p. 66).

⁶³ Smith, I, 186, 200.

⁶⁴ Prologue, *Every Man in His Humour* (quoted above, p. 12).

⁶⁵ As Professor Kittredge suggests (*As You Like It*, 1939, p. 126).

⁶⁶ Smith, I, 187.

[67] Smith, I, 200–201; *As You Like It*, IV, i, 18–33 (cf. Cook, p. 125).

[68] Cf. Collins, p. 102, and Eagle, *Baconiana*, XIII (1915), 154 ff.

[69] Smith, I, 199–200.

[70] *Much Ado About Nothing*, II, iii, 10–11.

[71] *Love's L. L.*, V, ii, 864–869.

[72] *All's Well That Ends Well*, III, vi, 43.

[73] *Merchant*, I, i, 80.

[74] *All's Well*, II, iv, 37–38.

[75] For discussion see above, pp. 53–55.

[76] Smith, I, 201–204.

[77] Cf. *Merry Wives of Windsor*, I, i, 205–206; "I had rather than forty shillings I had my Book of Songs and Sonnets here."

[78] "Which hang together," Sidney adds, "like a man which once told me the wind was at North West and by South, because he would be sure to name winds enow" (Smith, I, 201). Cook (p. 126) compares *Hamlet*, II, ii, 396–397: "I am but mad north-north-west. When the wind is southerly I know a hawk from a handsaw."

[79] *Timon*, V, i, 87–88. Cf. the contrast between the "high terms" and the "words sweetly placed and modestly directed" of *1 Henry VI*, I, ii, 93, and V, iii, 179; and Sonnet 86, "the proud full sail of his great verse."

[80] *Love's L. L.*, V, ii, 406–413.

[81] *Hamlet*, III, i, 51–53; cf. line 148: "I have heard of *your paintings* too, well enough"; and *Love's L. L.*, II, i, 13–14, IV, iii, 239 ("Fie, painted rhetoric"); *Measure for Measure*, IV, ii, 37–40; *Richard III*, I, iii, 241.

[82] *Love's L. L.*, I, i, 166–179; *Hamlet*, V, ii, 84, 137, 190–196.

[83] "A gift I have . . . full of forms, figures, shapes," *Love's L. L.*, IV, ii, 67.

[84] *Love's L. L.*, IV, ii, 57–59.

[85] Smith, I, 203.

[86] *1 Henry IV*, III, i, 125.

[87] Smith, I, 182.

[88] Cf. *King John*, IV, ii, 11–16:

> To gild refined gold, to paint the lily,
> To throw a perfume on the violet,
> To smooth the ice, or add another hue
> Unto the rainbow, or with taper light
> To seek the beauteous eye of heaven to garnish,
> Is wasteful and ridiculous excess.

[89] *I Henry IV*, III, ii, 72–73.

[90] In a letter (October 18, 1580) to his brother, Sidney had described "Ciceronianism" as "the chief abuse of Oxford" (*Miscellaneous Works*, ed. Gray, p. 337).

[91] Cook's note, p. 127, on Sidney's "sugar and spice": "Cf. Shakespeare's *As You Like It*, III, iii, 31"; i.e. Shakespeare's "honey a sauce to sugar."

[92] Smith, I, 202–203.

[93] *Epistle to Reynolds* (1627), quoted by Cook, p. 128.

[94] *Lear*, III, iv, 77; *Richard II*, II, i, 125–127.

[95] *Romeo and Juliet*, III, v, 31; *As You Like It*, II, i, 13–14.

[96] *I Henry IV*, II, iv, 441–455.

[97] A couple of intervening paragraphs of Sidney's, on versification ancient and modern, belong with his earlier discussion of poetic technique. This is reviewed in the next chapter.

[98] Smith, I, 204.

[99] Cook, p. 130.

[100] *Romeo and Juliet*, II, vi, 7; *Love's L. L.*, V, ii, 334; *Lear*, I, i, 201 (see Kittredge's note in his edition, 1940, p. 125); *I Henry IV*, II, iv, 268–269.

[101] Smith, I, 204.

[102] *I Henry IV*, III, i, 124; cf. Smith, I, 178.

[103] *Richard II*, I, iii, 309, 159–161.

CHAPTER III

[1] Plus — as indicated above, pp. 14–15, and notes to Chap. II — closely related material from other parts of the *Defense*.

[2] Smith, I, 151.

[3] Smith, I, 194, 193.

[4] Smith, I, 151.

[5] Smith, I, 195.

[6] Smith, I, 157, 195, 154.

[7] Smith, I, 184, 159.

[8] Smith, I, 153, 184.

[9] Smith, I, 154, 151. Cf. *A Midsummer N. D.*, I, i, 27–36, on the "cunning" charm of Lysander's bewitching rhymes; and *Two Gentlemen of Verona*, III, ii, 68–72.

[10] Smith, I, 151, 153, 151–152. For Shakespeare's version of this theme see above, p. 38.

[11] Smith, I, 151. Cf. "civil war of wits" (*Love's L. L.*, II, i, 226).

[12] Smith, I, 153.

[13] Smith, I, 182.

[14] "But if," Sidney continues, "you cannot hear the planet-like music of poetry . . . I will . . . wish . . . you . . . that . . . when you die, your memory die from the earth for want of an epitaph" (Smith, I, 156, 206–207).

[15] Cf. Spingarn, as quoted above, p. 13.

[16] In *The Tears of the Muses* and *The Shepherd's Calendar* (October).

[17] Concerning Dekker and Jonson see the former's Prologue to *If it Be Not Good* and his letter to Henslowe on September 12, 1616 (*Henslowe Papers*, ed. W. W. Greg, 1907, p. 92), and the latter's *Conversations* with Drummond (Shakespeare Society, London, 1842, p. 35; cf. Thaler, *Shakspere to Sheridan*, 1922, pp. 23–26, and nn.). On Daniel and Milton, cf. *Musophilus* and *Lycidas*, respectively.

[18] "And Tully's orator" (*Titus Andronicus*, IV, i, 14). Cf. Sidney on "sweet poesy," "sweet poetry" (Smith, I, 193, 179).

[19] *As You Like It*, I, i, 125; cf. above p. 35.

[20] *Two Gentlemen*, III, ii, 72; cf. above p. 34.

[21] "Music and poetry use to quicken you" (*Taming*, I, i, 36). Cf. *1 Henry IV*, III, i, 207–210; *Romeo and Juliet*, II, ii, 167–168; and *The Passionate Pilgrim*, VIII (though these lines may not be Shakespeare's):

> If music and sweet poetry agree,
> As they must needs (the sister and the brother).

Cf. above, p. 35.

[22] Sonnet 55. Cf. (on this page) n. 14, and *Hamlet*, II, ii, 546–551: "The players . . . are the abstract and brief chronicles of the time. After your death you were better have a bad epitaph than their ill report while you live."

[23] Smith, I, 200. (Cf. above, p. 34, and Chap. III, nn. 7 and 8.)

[24] *Othello*, I, iii, 290. On Sidney's use of Horace's *Ars Poetica*, see Smith, I, 166, 198, 390, 400.

[25] *Henry VIII*, IV, ii, 144.

[26] *Romeo and Juliet*, I, iii, 82.

[27] *Love's L. L.*, I, i, 112–113 (cf. I, i, 8–13, 70–93; IV, iii, 299–323). See also *2 Henry VI*, IV, vii, 78–79:

> Ignorance is the curse of God,
> Knowledge the wing wherewith we fly to heaven.

[28] *Romeo and Juliet,* III, iii, 160; *Taming,* I, ii, 160.

[29] Smith, I, 160.

[30] *As You Like It,* III, ii, 341.

[31] *Love's L. L.,* I, i, 74–87.

[32] *Love's L. L.,* IV, iii, 314–315.

[33] *Love's L. L.,* I, i, 58.

[34] *Merchant,* V, i, 79–80; *Two Gentlemen,* III, ii, 78–79.

[35] *Love's L. L.,* IV, iii, 348, 222. In thought and phrase, this passage is virtually identical with Sidney's statement quoted above, p. 35.

[36] Smith, I, 159–160, 206, 160, 182.

[37] *Antony and Cleopatra,* V; ii, 215; *1 Henry IV,* III, i, 130; *Henry V,* V, ii, 163; *Midsummer N. D.,* II, i, 67; *Julius Caesar,* III, iii, 32–35.

[38] Cf. Thaler, *Shakespeare and Democracy,* p. 79.

[39] *Henry V,* V, ii, 167; *Much Ado,* I, i, 254–255.

[40] *As You Like It,* III, ii, 178, 186, 101–105, 119.

[41] *1 Henry IV,* III, i, 133–135.

[42] *Julius Caesar,* IV, iii, 133; *King John,* IV, ii, 150; *Much Ado,* V, ii, 37; *Comedy of Errors,* II, ii, 49.

[43] *Troilus and Cressida,* IV, iv, 22; III, ii, 189; *Love's L. L.,* V, ii, 35; IV, iii, 322; Sonnet 79; *Timon,* I, i, 16; *As You Like It,* III, iv, 44; *1 Henry VI,* I, i, 27.

[44] In a somewhat different sense (*2 Henry IV,* IV, i, 23). But cf. *Richard II,* V, v, 43:

> How sour sweet music is
> When time is broke and no proportion kept.

[45] For Shakespearean notes on this theme see above, Chap. III, n. 21, and *Love's L. L.,* I, i, 168.

[46] Smith, I, 160, 182–183.

[47] *Titus,* IV, ii, 22–23.

[48] Smith, I, 195. (Cf. Horace, *Ars Poetica,* lines 408–411.)

[49] Thaler, *Shakespeare and Democracy,* pp. 62 ff.

[50] Sonnet 66.

[51] *Timon,* I, i, 20–22.

[52] *Hamlet,* II, ii, 120–121.

[53] *Much Ado,* V, ii, 30–36.

[54] Smith, I, 152.

[55] Smith, I, 154, and, for the passages next quoted, I, 195.

[56] *Love's L. L.,* IV, ii, 126–127.

[57] The poetaster in *Timon* (I, i, 32–38) flatters his fellow "artist" with the same large claim:

> How big imagination
> Moves in this lip. . . .
> It tutors nature. Artificial strife
> Lives in these touches, livelier than life.

Lear, in one of the pregnant denials of his madness, challenges this glibly conventional perversion of the principle:

> *Lear*: I am the King himself.
> *Edgar*: O thou side-piercing sight!
> *Lear*: *Nature's above art* in that respect.
>
> [IV, vi, 84–86.]

[58] Smith I, 154, 156.

[59] See above, pp. 8–9.

[60] Per contra, Richard II's queen insists that imagination fundamentally draws upon *known* experience:

> Conceit [imagination] is still derived
> From some forefather grief.
>
> [*Richard II*, II, ii, 34–35.]

[61] Smith, I, 157, 155.

[62] Man's superiority to "the works of . . . nature . . . in nothing he showeth so much as in poetry, when with the force of *a divine breath* he bringeth things forth far surpassing her doings" (Smith, I, 157).

[63] *Tempest*, IV, i, 151–158.

[64] See above, p. 18.

[65] Smith, I, 185.

[66] See above, pp. 19–21.

[67] *Midsummer N. D.*, V, i, 430; *Romeo and Juliet*, I, iv, 96–103.

[68] *Astrophel and Stella*, sonnets 5 and 45, glance at the subject, but are not real exceptions.

[69] See above, p. 9, and Chap. I, n. 26.

[70] *2 Henry IV*, I, iii, 31–32.

[71] *Twelfth Night*, II, v, 179.

[72] *Measure*, V, i, 406; *Lear*, IV, vi, 134.

[73] *Lear*, IV, vi, 290.

[74] *Lucrece*, lines 1422–1426.

[75] *Midsummer N. D.*, V, i, 21–22. Cf. *Hamlet*, III, iv, 114: "Conceit [imagination] in weakest bodies strongest works."

88

[76] *A Lover's Complaint*, lines 136–137.

[77] *Richard II*, I, iii, 294–299.

[78] *Timon*, I, i, 32–38; *2 Henry IV*, I, iii, 31; *Tempest*, II, i, 208; *Midsummer N. D.*, V, i, 18, 5; *Hamlet*, III, i, 128.

[79] Smith, I, 167.

[80] For discussion, cf. Thaler, *Shakespeare and Democracy*, pp. 82–83.

[81] *3 Henry VI*, I, ii, 31; cf. *Merchant*, V, i, 79.

[82] Smith, I, 168.

[83] Smith, I, 169, 168.

[84] Smith, I, 169.

[85] Smith, I, 160.

[86] *Timon*, I, i, 32–38 (quoted above, Chap. III, n. 57); *3 Henry VI*, IV, ii, 11; *Richard III*, V, i, 21; *Titus*, IV, iv, 21.

[87] *Twelfth Night*, I, v, 207–208; cf. Wordsworth, *Elegiac Stanzas*; and *Hamlet*, I, iv, 56.

[88] *As You Like It*, III, iii, 19–20; cf. *Midsummer N. D.*, V, i, 8.

[89] Sidney's preliminary mention of three *general* "kinds": religious, philosophical, and "indeed *right*" (i.e. creative) poetry, has little bearing upon Shakespeare.

[90] Smith, I, 159–160, 175.

[91] Smith, I, 175.

[92] Smith, I, 161, 175, 161.

[93] See above, p. 18.

[94] Smith, I, 175.

[95] See above, pp. 15–28.

[96] Smith, I, 175–176.

[97] "Shakespeare's Pastorals," *Studies in Philology*, XIII (1916), 122–154.

[98] See above, p. 6.

[99] *Measure*, IV, iii, 175.

[100] See above, p. 6, and Chap. I, n. 14.

[101] See above p. 18.

[102] *The Winter's Tale*, IV, iv, 134.

[103] *As You Like It*.

[104] Quoted above, on p. 51, and below, Chap. III, nn. 109, 110.

[105] *2 Henry IV*, III, i, 5–31.

[106] *Henry V*, IV, i, 283–297.

[107] *Cymbeline*, III, iii.

[108] *Love's L. L.*, V, ii, 913.

[109] *2 Henry IV*, III, i, 30–31. Cf. Alexander Iden's delight in his "quiet walks" in Kent, remote from the "turmoiled . . . court" (*2 Henry VI*, IV, x, 19).

[110] *3 Henry VI*, II, v, 88–98, 42–45.

[111] *Richard III*, II, ii, 67.

[112] Smith, I, 176; *Two Gentlemen*, III, ii, 82. Cf. *Titus*, III, ii, 46: "bitter deep laments."

[113] *Romeo and Juliet*, IV, v, 82; *Hamlet*, I, ii, 87.

[114] Smith, I, 186.

[115] *As You Like It*, III, ii, 379.

[116] *Cymbeline*, IV, ii, 193.

[117] *All's Well*, I, i, 64; cf. *Two Gentlemen*, III, i, 241: "Cease to lament for that thou canst not help."

[118] *Richard III*, IV, iv, 126.

[119] *Titus*, III, i, 219.

[120] *Romeo and Juliet*, IV, v, 49.

[121] *King John*, III, iv, 92; *Richard II*, IV, i, 193; III, iii, 164.

[122] Smith, I, 176.

[123] *Hamlet*, III, ii, 252; II, ii, 194–199; I, iii, 115. The "galled jade" was proverbially familiar before Shakespeare and Sidney (cf. *Hamlet*, ed. Kittredge, p. 227).

[124] *Midsummer N. D.*, V, i, 54.

[125] *As You Like It*, II, vii, 50–60.

[126] Smith, I, 178–179, 186, 201.

[127] Smith, I, 201. The rest of the passage is quoted above on p. 29.

[128] *Merry Wives*, I, i, 206: "I had rather than forty shillings I had my Book of Songs and Sonnets here."

[129] *Two Gentlemen*, III, ii, 68–69:

> Tangle her desires
> By wailful sonnets.

[130] *Love's L. L.*, III, i, 1.

[131] *As You Like It*, II, vii, 147–149.

[132] *Love's L. L.*, V, ii, 405.

[133] *Twelfth Night*, II, iv, 3, 43–49.

[134] Smith, I, 179–180.

[135] *Hamlet*, II, ii, 467–470.

[136] Smith, I, 161.

[137] See above, pp. 36–38.

[138] *Troilus*, IV, v, 202.

[139] For the following quotations from the *Defense*, see Smith, I, 161–162, 166, 163, 167, 190, 167, 190.

[140] *1 Henry IV*, II, iv, 500; *Troilus*, II, ii, 166–167; *2 Henry IV*, I, ii, 182–252.

[141] *As You Like It*, III, ii, 341; *Love's L. L.*, I, i, 74–87; IV, iii, 314–315 (quoted above on p. 37).

[142] The friar's "comfort" ("Adversity's sweet milk, philosophy") is cold comfort, according to Romeo (*Romeo and Juliet*, III, iii, 55–58). Cf. *Much Ado*, V, i, 31–36.

[143] Smith, I, 173, 171; *Two Gentlemen*, V, iv, 55; *3 Henry VI*, III, i, 34; *Merchant*, V, i, 84.

[144] Discussed above on pp. 69 ff.; cf. Smith, I, 190.

[145] *Timon*, I, i, 221–225.

[146] *Comus*, lines 476–478.

[147] *2 Henry VI*, IV, vii, 78–79.

[148] Smith, I, 191; *Love's L. L.*, I, i, 32–58, 113, 143; II, i, 23; IV, iii, 217; and the lines quoted above on pp. 37–38.

[149] *Henry V*, IV, vii, 98.

[150] Smith, I, 193, 171, 169.

[151] Smith, I, 169, 164.

[152] *2 Henry IV*, IV, i, 201–204. See also Sonnet 30: "And with old woes new wail my dear time's loss."

[153] See *Taming*, III, i, 81; *Love's L. L.*, I, i, 18; *Measure*, II, iv, 61; *2 Henry VI*, IV, vii, 16–17.

[154] Smith, I, 163, 167, 168.

[155] *2 Henry IV*, III, i, 80–84. Cf. *Measure*, I, i, 28–30:

> There is a kind of character in thy life
> That to th' observer doth thy history
> Fully unfold.

[156] Smith, I, 162.

[157] *Lear*, IV, vi, 153–154.

[158] On the "dust and injury of age" and "dry antiquity" in "ancient writers," cf. Sonnet 108, *As You Like It*, IV, iii, 106, and *1 Henry IV*, II, iv, 455.

[159] *Henry V*, II, iv, 86–87.

[160] *All's Well*, II, iii, 14.

[161] *Love's L. L.*, I, i, 74–87.

[162] In *Troilus* (IV, v, 202), Nestor is likened to a

> Good old chronicle
> That hast so long walk'd hand in hand with time.

In *Henry VIII* (IV, ii, 72), Queen Katherine describes Griffith "an honest chronicler."

[163] *Henry V*, I, ii, 163. Cf. *1 Henry IV*, V, ii, 57–58 (Vernon reporting how generously Prince Hal had eulogized Hotspur):

> Trimm'd up your praises with a princely tongue;
> Spoke your deservings like a chronicle.

[164] *Henry VIII*, I, ii, 72–74. In another section of the *Defense*, Sidney writes: "As in *history*, looking for truth," men "go away *full fraught with falsehood*, so in poesy, looking for fiction, they shall" find what amounts to "imaginative" truth (Smith, I, 185).

[165] Smith, I, 152–153, 162.

[166] *Richard III*, III, i, 69–79.

[167] *Lear*, I, i, 238–240.

[168] *Winter's Tale*, III, ii, 36–38.

[169] The quotations from Sir Philip in the following paragraph are from Smith, I, 168, 170, 167, 164, 169–170, 168–169, 170.

[170] See above, pp. 42–48.

[171] *Antony and Cleopatra*, II, v, 77.

[172] *Henry V*, Chorus, V, 1–2, 23.

[173] *1 Henry VI*, II, iv.

[174] *Richard II*, III, iv.

[175] Smith, I, 166.

CHAPTER IV

[1] Smith, I, 181–193. For the phrases next quoted see Smith, I, 193.

[2] *Hamlet*, II, ii, 343–368.

[3] Smith, I, 182–183.

[4] See above, pp. 38–42, and Smith, I, 182.

[5] Smith, I, 183 ff.

[6] Cf. *Complete Shakespeare*, Kittredge ed., pp. 229, 160; Thaler, *Shakespeare and Democracy*, pp. 106 ff.

[7] *Love's L. L.*, I, i, 13.

[8] Smith, I, 190–192.

[9] See above, pp. 55–58.

[10] Smith, I, 190.

[11] See above, pp. 57–58.

[12] Smith, I, 184. Cf. above, pp. 57, 17.

[13] Smith, I, 184–185.

[14] *Henry V*, Prologue, 11–14; cf. above, p. 44.

[15] Smith, I, 185–186; cf. above, p. 9.

[16] See above, p. 58.

[17] *Timon*, I, i, 226–228.

[18] *As You Like It* (1939), III, iii, 26–27, and p. xvi.

[19] See above, p. 47.

[20] *As You Like It*, III, iii, 19. I have written elsewhere that "in . . . many passages Shakespeare . . . plays upon the secondary meaning of *feign*, in the sense of pretend or sham (e.g. 'most friendship is feigning'). But there can be no doubt that, beneath the jest, he knew and in his remarks on poetry meant to press seriously the primary sense of *feigning* — i.e., bodying forth, imagining (as in 'all that poets feign of bliss and joy'), which Sir Philip Sidney in his *Apology* had authoritatively set down as the very essence of poetry" (Thaler, *Shakespeare and Democracy*, pp. 82–83).

[21] Smith, I, 186–189.

[22] See above, pp. 52–55.

[23] Shakespeare's variant; cf. previous n.

[24] Smith, I, 186–187.

[25] This observation may be compared with Sidney's earlier antithesis (Smith, I, 167) between "true matters, such as *indeed* were done, and not such as *fantastically* . . . may be suggested"; and that, in turn with Banquo's query:

> Are ye fantastical, or that indeed
> Which outwardly ye show?
> > [*Macbeth*, I, iii, 53–54; cf. Cook, p. 85.]

[26] See above, p. 8; and cf. *Much Ado*, II, iii, 22: "His words are a very fantastical banquet."

[27] See *Romeo and Juliet*, I, iv, 98; *Twelfth Night*, I, i, 15.

[28] Smith, I, 187–188.

[29] Cf. *Henry VIII*, III, ii, 386; *Hamlet*, V, ii, 95.

[30] For example:

> Fair use
> Revolts from true birth, stumbling on abuse.
> > [*Romeo and Juliet*, II, iii, 19–20.]

Also *Lear*, I, iii, 20; *Richard III*, I, iii, 52; *Love's L. L.*, II, i, 227; *Measure*, II, i, 43; Sonnet 82.

[31] *Merchant*, III, ii, 75–79; cf. *Lear*, IV, vi, 153–177; Smith, I, 187.

[32] Smith, I, 187–189.

[33] *Hamlet*, III, i, 88.

[34] See above, p. 37; Smith, I, 187–188.

[35] Smith, I, 189, 188.

[36] *1 Henry IV*, III, i, 167, 190; cf. above, p. 39.

[37] *Hamlet*, II, ii, 120–121: "I am ill at these numbers; I have not the art to reckon my groans," etc.

[38] Cf. Thaler, *Shakespeare and Democracy*, p. 79.

[39] Rupert Taylor, PMLA, LI (1936), 643, n. 3; cf. G. C. Taylor, *Philological Quarterly*, XXII (1943), 330 ff.

[40] See above, p. 9.

[41] W. Farrand, Introduction to *The Princess* (New York, 1919), p. vii.

[42] Cf. Thaler, *Shakespeare's Silences* (1929), p. 115.

[43] "I never read . . . saw, nor heard" of Marlowe's *Faustus* (quoted by John Bakeless, *Christopher Marlowe*, 1937, p. 152).

[44] *Collected Works*, ed. May Morris (1910–1915), III, xviii.

[45] *Eikonoklastes*, chap. XXIII (*Prose Works*, ed. St. John, I, 458).

[46] See above, p. 10.

[47] "Marlowe's talent, like that of most poets, was partly synthetic" (T. S. Eliot, *Selected Essays*, London, 1932, pp. 119–120).

[48] Bakeless, p. 173. Thus, for example, Marlowe's famous line in *Dr. Faustus*, "Was this the face that launched a thousand ships . . .?" is echoed and reëchoed in Shakespeare's *Richard II*, IV, i, 281–286:

> Was this . . . the face
> That every day under his household roof
> Did keep ten thousand men? Was this the face
> That like the sun did make beholders wink?
> Was this the face that fac'd so many follies
> And was at last outfac'd by Bolingbroke?

And the echo grows even closer in *Troilus*, II, ii, 81–82, where Helen is described as

> a pearl
> Whose price hath launch'd above a thousand ships.

[49] Cf. H. O. White, *Plagiarism and Imitation During the English Renaissance* (1935), p. 108.

INDEX

Adams, J. Q., 78(n.35), 82(n. 53)

Alexander the Great, 71

Anders, H. R. D., 75(n.6)

Anderson, Maxwell, *Winterset*, 74

Aristotle, 3, 25–26, 64, 71

Arnold, Matthew, 8

Ascham, Roger, *The Schoolmaster*, 3, 75(n.1)

Bacon, Sir Francis, 33; "Of Truth," 46

Bakeless, John, 74, 93(nn.43, 48)

Boethius, 57

Bond, W. H., 75(n.7), 77(n. 34), 78(n.42)

Browne, Sir Thomas, 73, 93(n. 42)

Bruller, Jean (*pseudonym*: Vercors), 46

Byron, George Gordon, Lord, viii, 73, 93(n.43)

Caesar, Julius, 18, 63

Camden, William, 76(n.16)

Carlyle, Thomas, 4

Cato, 40

Chambers, E. K., 6, 75(n.6), 76(n.16)

Chaucer, 33, 41, 67; *Troilus*, 41, 79(n.5)

Churchyard, Thomas, 11, 77 (n.34)

Cicero, 3, 17, 80(n.20), 85(n. 18); Ciceronianism, 31, 84 (n.90)

Coleridge, Samuel Taylor, 8, 19

Collins, J. C., 75(nn.7–8), 76 (n.18), 83(n.68)

Connolly, Cyril, 80(n.15)

Cook, A. S., 3, 7, 9, 32, 75(nn. 7, 9), 76(nn.18, 21, 23), 77(nn.27, 33–34), 79(nn. 1–2), 82(n.44), 83(nn.67, 78), 84(nn.91, 93, 99), 92 (n.25)

Croft, H. H. S., 80(nn.10, 20)

Daniel, Samuel, 33, 36, 74, 85 (n.17)

Dares Phrygius, 47

Dekker, Thomas, 36, 85(n.17)

Demosthenes, 3

Dionysius of Halicarnassus, 76 (n.16)

Donatus, 80(n.20)

Douce, F., 76(n.16)

Drayton, Michael, 11, 31–33, 77(n.34), 84(n.93)

Eagle, R., 80(n.22), 83(n.68)

Eliot, T. S., 74, 93(n.47)

Elyot, Sir Thomas, 80(nn.10, 20)

Emerson, Ralph Waldo, 4

Erasmus, 3

Euclid, 73

Euphuism, 31

Fables of Bidpai, The, 76(n.17)
Farnham, W. E., 79(n.5)
Farrand, W., 93(n.41)
Feuillerat, A., 75(n.7)
Florio, John, 11
Flügel, E., 17, 75(n.7), 80(n. 18)
Fuller, Thomas, 78(n.35)
Furness, H. H., 6, 75(n.7), 76 (nn.16–17)

Gascoigne, George, 22, 82(n.50)
George III, viii
Gorboduc, 17, 76(n.20), 80(n. 17)
Gosson, Stephen, 14, 66
Gower, John, 79(n.5)
Gray, William, 76(n.12), 77(n. 32), 84(n.90)
Greenlaw, E., 50, 77(n.34), 88 (n.97)
Greg, W. W., 85(n.17)

Harington, Sir John, 5, 11, 75 (n.10)
Henslowe, Philip, 85(n.17)
Herford, C. H., 78(nn.38, 40, 42)
Homer, 71
Horace, 36, 40; *Ars Poetica*, 9, 77(n.28), 82(n.44), 85(n. 24), 86(n.48)
Hunter, E. R., ix

Johnson, Samuel, ix; *Preface to Shakespeare*, 20, 81(n.37); *Rasselas*, viii, 72
Jonson, Ben, 11–13, 17, 26, 36, 40, 66, 78(n.34); *Conversations* with Drummond, 85

(n.17); *Every Man in His Humour*, 11–12, 78(n.40) 82(n.64); *Poetaster*, 11, 78 (n.38); *Silent Woman*, 11– 12, 78(n.42); *Timber*, 11 78(n.37); *Volpone*, 80(n 23)

Kemp, Will, 10
King Cambyses, 18, 24
Kittredge, George Lyman, 18– 19, 69, 76(n.22), 79(n.5), 80(n.12), 81(n.34), 82(n 65), 89(n.123), 91(n.6)
Klein, David, 75(n.7), 81(n 40), 82(n.62)

Leicester's Men, Earl of, 10
Livy, 47, 76(n.16)
Lyly, John, 31

Marlowe, Christopher, 74, 93 (n.47); *Dr. Faustus*, 93 (nn.43, 48); *Hero and Le- ander*, 41, 48
Masefield, John, 33
Mathew, Frank, 22, 78(n.38), 82(n.49)
Meres, Francis, 11
Milton, John, 4, 36; *Comus*, 58, 90(n.146); *Eikonoclastes* 15, 73, 79–80(n.7), 93(n 45); *Lycidas*, 85(n.17)
Mirror for Magistrates, The 79(n.5)
Morris, May, 93(n.44)
Morris, William, 73, 93(n.44)
Munn, James B., ix
Myrick, K. O., 79(n.1)

Nashe, Thomas, 11, 78(n.34)
North, Sir Thomas, 76(nn.16–17)

Oedipus, 16
Osgood, C. G., 77(n.34)

Padelford, F. M., 77–78(n.34)
Percy and Douglas, ballad of, 54–55
Piozzi, Hester Lynch (Mrs. Thrale), ix
Plato, 3, 36, 42, 57–58, 67–69, 71
Plautus, 18, 80(n.26); *Amphitruo*, 23
Plutarch, 76(n.16)
Puttenham, George, 11

Quiller-Couch, Sir Arthur, 76 (n.12)

Raleigh, Sir Walter, 77(n.34)
Roberts, S. C., ix
Rollins, Hyder E., ix, 79(n.5)

St. John, J. A., 80(n.7), 93(n. 45)
Schelling, F. E., 78(n.37), 79 (n.5)
Schlegel, A. W., 19
Seneca, 18, 80(n.26)
Shakespeare, William, Plays:
    All's Well That Ends Well, 27–28, 52, 61, 83(nn.72, 74), 89(n.117), 90(n. 160)
    Antony and Cleopatra, 19, 39, 48, 55, 64–65, 81(n.33), 86(n.37), 91(n.171)
    As You Like It, 25–28, 32,

37, 39, 47–48, 51–54, 57, 69, 82(n.65), 83(n. 67), 84(nn.91, 95), 85 (n.19), 86(nn.30, 40, 43), 88(nn.88, 103), 89 (nn.115, 125, 131), 90 (nn.141, 158), 92(nn. 18, 20)
    Comedy of Errors, 86(n.42)
    Coriolanus, 5–6, 48, 50, 76 (n.16), 88(n.101)
    Cymbeline, 23, 51–52, 88(n. 107), 89(n.116)
    Hamlet, 7, 16–18, 21–22, 24, 28, 30, 36, 41, 46, 49–50, 52–53, 55, 58, 71, 74, 80(nn.12, 20, 22–23), 81(nn.27, 31), 82 (nn. 45, 47), 83(nn.78, 81–82), 85(n.22), 86 (n.52), 87(n.75), 88(nn. 78, 87, 101); 89(nn.113, 123, 135), 91(n.2), 92 (n.129), 93(nn.33, 37)
    1 Henry IV, 23–24, 28, 31–32, 39, 41, 56, 64–65, 71, 82(n.54), 83(n.86), 84(nn.89, 96, 100, 102), 85(n.21), 86(nn.37, 41), 90(nn.140, 158), 91(n. 163), 93(n.36)
    2 Henry IV, 7, 23, 25, 27–28, 45–46, 51, 56, 59–60, 62, 64–65, 76(n.20), 80 (n.9), 81(n.33), 86(n. 44), 87(n.70), 88(nn. 78, 105), 89(n.109), 90 (nn.140, 152, 155)
    Henry V, 16, 19–20, 23, 27–28, 39, 44, 51, 59, 61–62,

65, 68, 80(n.14), 81(nn. 35–36, 38), 86(nn.37, 39), 88(n.106), 90(nn. 149, 159), 91(nn.163, 172, 14)

1 Henry VI, 65, 81(n.33), 83(n.79), 86(n.43), 91 (n.173)

2 Henry VI, 51, 58–59, 85(n. 27), 88(n.104), 89(n. 109), 90(nn. 147, 153)

3 Henry VI, 46–47, 51, 77(n. 23), 82(n.62), 88(nn.81, 86, 104), 89(n.110), 90 (n.143)

Henry VIII, 36, 62, 85(n.25), 91(nn.162, 164), 92(n. 29)

Julius Caesar, 55, 86(nn.37, 42)

King John, 31, 39, 52, 65, 83(n.88), 86(n.42), 89 (n.121)

King Lear, 4, 21, 23, 32, 45, 61, 63, 82(nn.45, 59), 84 (nn.94, 100), 87(nn. 57, 72–73), 90(n.157), 91(n.167), 92(nn.30–31)

Love's Labour's Lost, 5, 16, 21, 25, 27–32, 37–39, 42, 48, 51, 54–55, 57–58, 61, 67, 76(n.12), 80 (n.13), 82(n.57), 83 (nn.71, 80–84), 84(n. 100), 85(nn.11, 27), 86 (nn. 31–33, 35, 43, 45, 56), 88(n.108), 89(nn. 130, 132), 90(nn.141, 148, 153, 161), 91(n.7), 92(n.30)

Macbeth, 9, 16, 64, 80(n. 16), 81(n.33), 92(n.25)

Measure for Measure, 23, 45, 50, 83(n.81), 87(n.72), 88(n.99), 90(nn.153, 155), 92(n.30)

Merchant of Venice, 7, 38, 70–71, 76–77(n.23), 82(n. 45), 83(n.73), 86(n. 34), 88(n.81), 90(n. 143), 92(n.31)

Merry Wives of Windsor, 54, 83(n. 77), 89(n.128)

Midsummer Night's Dream, 8, 9, 24, 28, 36, 39, 42–48, 53, 82(n.61), 84(n.9), 86(n.37), 87(nn.67, 75), 88(nn.78, 88), 89 (n. 124)

Much Ado About Nothing, 27–28, 39, 41, 57, 83(n. 70), 86(nn. 39, 42, 53), 90(n. 142), 92(n.26)

Othello, 36, 48, 64, 77(n.23), 85(n.24)

Pericles, 79(n.5), 81(n.40)

Richard II, 23, 32, 45, 52, 64–65, 84(nn.94, 103), 86(n.44), 87(n.60), 88 (n.77), 89(n.121), 91 (n.174), 93(n.48)

Richard III, 15, 23, 47, 52, 63–64, 79(n.7), 80(nn. 9, 10), 82(n.52), 83(n. 81), 88(n.86), 89(nn. 111, 118), 91(n.166), 92(n.30)

Romeo and Juliet, 27, 32, 37, 44, 48, 52, 55, 57, 70–71, 74, 81(n.39), 84(nn.95,

100), 85(nn.21, 26), 86
(n.28), 87(n.67), 89
(nn.113, 120), 90(n.
142), 92(nn.27, 30)

Taming of the Shrew, 25, 28,
37–38, 58, 82(nn.56,
60), 85(n.21), 86(n.
28), 90(n.153)

Tempest, The, 43, 46, 87(n.
63), 88(n.78)

Timon of Athens, 29, 41, 46–
47, 57–58, 68–69, 81(n.
41), 83(n.79), 86(nn.
43, 51), 87(n.57), 88
(nn.78, 86), 90(n.145),
92(n.17)

Titus Andronicus, 40, 47, 55,
85(n.18), 86(n.47), 88
(n.86), 89(nn.112, 119)

Troilus and Cressida, 23, 25,
55–56, 62, 86(n.43), 89
(n.138), 90(nn.140,
162), 93(n.48)

Twelfth Night, 25, 28, 45,
47, 55, 70, 80(n.17), 87
(n.71), 88(n.87), 89
(n. 133), 92(n.27)

Two Gentlemen of Verona,
36, 52, 54, 57, 84(n.9),
85(n.20), 86(n.34), 89
(nn.112, 117, 129), 90
(n.143)

Winter's Tale, 20–21, 27, 44,
51, 64, 88(n.102), 91
(n.168)

Shakespeare, William, Poems:
Lover's Complaint, A, 45,
88(n.76). *Passionate Pilgrim*, 85(n.21). *Rape of
Lucrece*, 45, 87(n.74).

Sonnets, 4, 29, 36, 40, 44,
54, 61, 74, 83(n.79), 85
(n.22), 86(nn.43, 50), 90
(nn.152, 158), 92(n.
30). On dramatic and
poetic technique, principles,
"kinds," etc., *see* Sidney,
Defense of Poesy

Shelley, Percy Bysshe, viii, 8–10,
74, 77(nn.29, 30)

Shuckburgh, E. S., 75(n.7), 77
(n.33), 79(n.2), 80(nn.
10, 20), 81(n.35)

Sidney, Sir Philip, 71, 73. *Arcadia*, 4, 10, 28, 31, 74.
Astrophel and Stella, 4, 7,
10, 29, 45, 54, 80(n.18),
87(n.68). *Defense of
Poesy*, 2; editions of, 3, 75
(nn.1, 7); major principles
illustrated by Shakespeare's
practice, 4; major divisions,
14; analysis (with pertinent
Shakespearian allusions or
illustrations) of the function of tragedy, 15–18; differentiation of "kinds," 17–
18; "laws," 18–21; proprieties, 21–22; tragicomedy,
18, 22–24; comedy, definition and function, 24–26;
abuse and right use, 26–27;
comic laughter, 27–28, 78
(n.40); extravagant dic-
tion, 28–30; "letter-coursing," 30; Ciceronians and
Euphuists, 31–32; the English language, 32–33; po-
etry's low estate and divine
origin, 34–36; immortal

garlands, 35–36; ethical-aesthetic function, 36–38; relation to verse and rhyme, 38–40; need of industry plus genius, 40–42; poetry and creative imagination, 42–48; poetic "parts, kinds or species," 48–50; the pastoral, 50–51; elegiac, 52; satiric, 53; lyric, 53–55; heroic, 55; poetry and philosophy, 55–58; poetry and history, 47, 58–65; "poet-haters" refuted: on rhyme and verse, 66–67; Plato's attack answered, 67–68; poetry the most "fruitful" knowledge, 68; not "the mother of lies," 44, 46, 68–69; not the "nurse" of sin, 67, 69–70; right use versus "fantastic" abuse, 70–71; *passim.*

Simpson, P., 78(nn.38, 40, 42)

Smith, G. Gregory, 75(n.10), 78(n.40); ed. of Sidney's *Defense,* 10; 75(nn.1, 7, 9, 11), 76(nn.13–14, 18); *passim.*

Spenser, Edmund, 3, 11, 33, 36, 67, 74, 77–78(n.34); *Mother Hubbard's Tale,* 50; *Shepherd's Calendar,* 50, 79(n.5), 85(n.16); *Tears of the Muses,* 85(n.16)

Spingarn, J. E., 11, 13, 18, 78 (n.37), 79(n.43), 80(n.20), 81(n.30), 85(n.15)

Surrey, Henry Howard, Earl of, 79(n.5)

Taylor, G. C., 75(n.2), 93(n.39)

Taylor, Rupert, 73, 93(n.39)

Tennyson, Alfred, Lord, 73–74, 93(n.41)

Thaler, Alwin, 75(n.7), 77(n.24), 79(n.5), 81(n.35), 85(n.17), 86(nn.38, 49), 88(n.80), 91(n.6), 92(n.20), 93(nn.38, 42)

Thrale, Mrs., *see* Piozzi, Hester Lynch

Tillyard, E. M. W., 78(n.36)

Tottel, Richard, 54

Tottel's Miscellany, 29, 54, 83 (n.77), 89(n.128)

Vaughan, Henry, 11, 77(n.34)

Vercors, *see* Bruller, Jean

Virgil, 40, 47, 55, 69, 89(nn.134–135)

Walsingham, Sir Francis, 10

Whetstone, George, 82(n.50)

White, H. O., 93(n.49)

White, N. I., 9, 77(nn.29, 30)

Wilson, J. Dover, 76(n.12), 82 (n.58)

Wither, George, 11, 77(n.34)

Wordsworth, William, 8; *Elegiac Stanzas,* 47, 88(n.87); *Tintern Abbey,* viii

Xenophon, 47